First-Chance Exception

A Tale of Games, Gaffes, and Going Online

Raymond Arifianto

"Made me laugh. More than once."

- MARK MANDEL, Game Developer Advocate,
Founder of Agones and Quilkin projects

"We spend hundreds and thousands of hours playing our favorite video games, but most have no idea how they are made. First Class Exception tells a realistic behind-the-scenes story about the not-always-pretty way game developers build the games we love so much."

- MIKE FISCHER, Interactive Media Executive, Advisor and
Educator
(Microsoft, Amazon, Square Enix, Epic Games)

"Humorous, fast-paced and nostalgia-inducing. It had me reliving all those gut-wrenching WTF moments that make up the madness and passion that is real game development."

- PHIL TOSSELL, Game Creator
(AccelByte, Microsoft, Rare)

"A fun narrative about video game development, whether you've been part of a similar journey or just interested in the chaos that engineering teams have to go through to ship their games. I found myself connecting with the characters, chuckling every once in a while and felt terrified in some of the early decisions as I could foresee how they were going to develop."

- ISAIAS FORMACIO-SERNA, Engineering
(Rec Room, PlayStation, Xbox)

"OMG! What an amazing way to mix storytelling and game industry insider experience! :) "

- SUMEET JAKATDAR, Technical Director
(Sony, Amazon Game Studios, Treyarch)

PUBLISHED BY: Raymond Arifianto

EDITED BY: Jessica Arifianto

FIRST EDITION February 14, 2025

LAST UPDATED March 15, 2025 (V10)

ISBN 978-1-0693717-0-6

PREFACE

Hey there! Thanks for picking up this book—it means a lot to me!

My wife (who's also my editor) asked me why I wrote this book.

The simple answer is that game development has always been close to my heart, and one way or another, hijinks always find their way into the process. I've learned that life becomes a lot more entertaining when we don't take ourselves too seriously, especially in an industry where server launches are considered successful if nothing catches fire.

But there's another reason. The world's been a pretty intense place lately.

So I hoped that by sharing these stories—both the triumphs and the "well, that definitely happened" moments—I might bring a few chuckles into your day.

As a reminder, this is purely a work of fiction. Names, characters, businesses, places, events, locales, and incidents are either the products of the author's imagination or used in a fictitious manner. Any resemblance to actual persons, living or dead, or actual events is purely coincidental.

And no, you cannot actually refactor an entire game backend in six months and make it production ready. Not even with unlimited coffee, energy drinks, and philosophically sentient AI.

Game development is a complex, collaborative endeavor that requires teams of dedicated professionals working together over extended periods. While this story compresses timelines for narrative purposes, real game development involves careful planning, extensive testing, and countless iterations. Also, there are significantly more meetings about horse armor than depicted here.

If you're considering turning your single-player game into an always-online experience, please consult your local game backend engineer, server infrastructure team, and therapy group first.

No horses, rabbits, or servers were harmed in the making of this book.

(The AI's existential crises were purely fictional. Probably.)

thanks

Alexander Vlahopoulos

Adam Shetler

Mark Mandel

Phil Tossell

Sumeet Jakatdar

Isaias Formacio-Serna

Mark Fischer

Rebekah Mullen

Joseph Yan

Anggoro "Dewa" Dewanto

Rob Schoeppe

For Jessica, Drake and Ivy
Your love and patience made this possible

Table of Contents

PROLOGUE

Regalia Games: From Industry Pioneer to Last Chance at Redemption

Date: 2018 March 20 18:06 | Posted By: Rachel Thorne

Category > Technology

Two decades ago, Regalia Games revolutionized action-adventure gaming with MonArc, a masterpiece that redefined player expectations for open-world experiences. Today, that same studio faces potential closure, its future hanging by a thread as it prepares for one final gambit.

The original MonArc wasn't just successful – it was transformative. Its intricate world-building and groundbreaking gameplay mechanics earned both critical acclaim and a *BAFTA Games Award*,[1] establishing Regalia as an industry leader. The follow-up, MonArc II, proved lightning could strike twice, building thoughtfully on its predecessor's foundation while pushing boundaries further.

But the passing of time has not been kind to Regalia Games. The studio's slow decline reached its nadir with MonArc Journey, an ill-conceived Kinect exclusive that traded the franchise's depth for motion-controlled horse riding. Its sequel, the aptly titled MonArc Journey: No Horsing Around, doubled down on the gimmick, leaving players literally shouting at their screens in frustration. Industry whispers suggest a contractual obligation with Microsoft prompted the development of these titles, though the promised third installment may mercifully remain unreleased.

---

[1] **BAFTA Games Award:** Basically, the Oscars for video games, but with more tea and crumpets. Think "fancy British people giving golden masks to games" instead of "fancy Hollywood people giving golden statues to movies."

Now under the wing of Serious Business Games (SBG)—a publisher more renowned for its profit margins than creative vision—Regalia has announced its last shot at survival: MonArc Rebooted Verse (MARV). This always-online reimagining of the original MonArc represents everything the studio once stood against, trading intimate single-player storytelling for live service monetization.

SBG's recent announcement of a Fall 2019 release window, with playable demos planned for E3 2019, has only intensified fan outcry. "They've lost their way," wrote one Reddit user in a viral post. "MonArc was special because it respected players' time and money. MARV is just following trends."

The timing couldn't be more poignant. As MonArc's 25th anniversary approaches, the studio that crafted it struggles to justify transforming their masterpiece into what many view as a cynical cash grab. The decision to pursue MARV instead of a straightforward remaster of the beloved original has left long-time fans feeling betrayed.

E3 2019 looms as a crucial moment for both MARV and Regalia Games. The industry's premier showcase has launched legends and buried dreams in equal measure. For Regalia, it represents more than just another demo—it's potentially their final chance to prove they still understand what made MonArc special.

Should MARV fail, it threatens not only the studio's survival but also MonArc's legacy. The thought that this revered franchise might be remembered not for its groundbreaking origins but for a series of misguided experiments and a controversial online reboot has hardcore fans already mourning what once was.

As the clock ticks down to E3, the question isn't just whether MARV will succeed, but whether Regalia Games—a studio that once defined excellence in single-player game design—can survive its transformation into something entirely different. For a company that built its reputation on crafting intimate, personal experiences, the irony of betting everything on an always-online future isn't lost on anyone.

The gaming industry's history is littered with beloved studios that failed to adapt to changing times. Whether Regalia Games joins that list or pulls off an eleventh-hour resurrection may depend entirely on whatever they show at E3. One thing is certain: for better or worse, MARV represents more than just another game launch—it's the last stand of a once-great studio fighting for its very survival.

PART ONE:
E3 DEMO – BLOOD, SWEAT, AND CPU CYCLES

RAYMOND ARIFIANTO

18

Chapter 1:
Welcome to the Jungle

Early August 2018, T-minus less than 11 months to E3 2019

Timothy Casey's keycard still worked. That was a surprise.

Watching the familiar green LED blink to life, Tim smiled at a wave of nostalgia. Ten years in eCommerce had taught him a lot about building scalable systems and turning chaos into order, but it hadn't quite filled the void left by game development. Sure, optimizing shopping carts paid better than optimizing frame rates, but it lacked a certain magic.

Tim had acquired what he called his "eCommerce scars" during his decade away - strands of premature gray in his dark hair that appeared after particularly spectacular Black Friday disasters, smile lines earned from explaining to executives why they couldn't just "add more servers." His well-worn laptop bag bore stickers from a dozen different tech conferences, each representing a crisis survived or a system scaled. He had the measured calm of someone who had seen too many production servers catch fire to panic easily anymore.

"We never deleted you from the system," a British-accented voice called out. "Figured you'd be back eventually. Gamers always come back."

Benjamin Blackwood—Ben to everyone except his mother and the tax authorities—stood in the doorway, a maze of monitor cables draped over his shoulder. The engine and tools lead hadn't changed much in ten years: same dark blonde ponytail, same wire-rimmed glasses, same look of someone who had recently argued with a physics engine and won.

As the architect of Regalia's game engine, Ben spent his days crafting the tools that let artists create worlds and helping other programmers bend reality without breaking it entirely. The fact that Regalia's games ran at all was largely due to his ability to make impossible things merely improbable.

"Speaking of coming back," Ben continued, pushing his glasses up with his free hand, "fair warning about the all-hands meeting in ten. Mitch wants to talk about 'exciting new features.'" His air quotes could have cut glass.

"Mitch being...?"

"Mitch Holloway. Our new overlord from Serious Business Games. Executive Producer. The kind of guy who says, 'monetization strategy' more often than 'good morning.'" Ben's expression suggested the arrival of Mitch had been about as welcome as a memory leak in a physics simulation. "He's got quite the reputation and worked on some big franchises. Now he's here to ensure we don't waste any more of the publisher's money on wild experiments."

Tim had heard about SBG's acquisition of Regalia during one of their monthly game dev pub meetups. It was Jennifer Kovac who'd first hinted they needed help, cursing eloquently about their struggles with the transition to always-online gaming between sips of her craft IPA.

Jennifer 'Jen' Kovac was Regalia's technical producer and resident data wizard, a former competitive gamer whose intensity behind dual monitors betrayed her esports background. Her mechanical keyboard from her pro gaming days still clattered with machine-gun precision as she coordinated multiple team channels simultaneously. She'd earned the nickname "The Closer" during her competitive gaming career for clutch performances under pressure, but these days it referred to her legendary ability to identify exactly which features needed to be cut to ship a game on time.

The rapid-fire efficiency that once made her a feared opponent on the European esports circuit now made her an invaluable technical producer, even if her vocabulary still carried echoes of those late-night tournament streams. The fact that she was struggling with their current project was not a good sign.

"How's the backend looking?" Tim asked, setting up his laptop. "The contractor—Bruno, right?"

Ben's expression could have curdled milk. "Eleven months of the most beautiful, elaborate, totally unusable code you've ever seen. Pretty sure he implemented his own programming language at one point. Called it *BrunoScript*."

"That bad?"

"Let's just say your eCommerce experience will come in handy. Though selling horse armor is a bit different than selling shoes."

Before Tim could unpack that cryptic warning, a familiar string of creative profanity announced Jen's arrival. "Tim! Thank fuck you're here. Mitch's about to tell us how we need player housing. In a game where you're constantly riding across the continent. Player. Housing."

"The good news is the server might crash before we have to implement it," came a heavy Quebecois accent from the doorway. Guillaume Dubois, Regalia's principal gameplay engineer, joined them with a resigned smile. The man responsible for MonArc's famously unpredictable AI system—which was revolutionary partly because even Guillaume himself couldn't fully explain how it worked—looked like he'd been having several long days in a row.

21

Fittingly, Guillaume looked exactly like someone who spent his days teaching AI to question existence - his wild, curly hair seemed to defy both gravity and reason, as if reflecting the chaos of his neural networks. His desk was a maze of whiteboards covered in mathematical formulas and philosophical quotes, and he had the intense, slightly manic energy of someone who regularly debated consciousness with his own code. His Montreal Canadiens coffee mug had seen him through countless late-night AI debugging sessions, though these days it seemed to contain more Red Bull than coffee.

The all-hands was being held in what used to be their motion capture studio. Tim noticed Mitch Holloway immediately: sharp suit, sharper smile, the kind of presence that suggested someone used to steering billion-dollar franchises. Three years of development hell and multiple restarts had led SBG to install him as their on-site insurance policy.

Mitch stood at the front, clicking through a PowerPoint deck titled "MARV: Road to E3 2019 - Expanding Our Vision."

"Engagement metrics show players want more social features," Mitch was saying. "So, we're adding player housing, a marketplace, and a companion app–"

"*Calice,*"[2] Guillaume muttered. "The horses still clip through mountains."

"–and of course, expanded customization options for user generated content–"

---

[2] **Calice:** A French Canadian swear word derived from the Catholic communion chalice, roughly equivalent to '%#@!' but with more cultural flavor.

Tim's attention drifted to the technical architecture diagram on the screen. His natural inclination toward making lists kicked in as he started cataloging the challenges ahead. The backend system looked less like a service architecture and more like a Jackson Pollock painting. He counted at least three different database technologies, something labeled "BrunoCache™," and what appeared to be a custom-built message queue because Bruno apparently didn't trust *Kafka*.[3]

"All of this needs to be ready for E3," Mitch concluded. "Our E3 demo will showcase everything that makes MARV unique: seamless multiplayer, dynamic world events, player-driven economy–"

"Question," Tim raised his hand. "About the backend–"

"The backend is solid," Mitch waved him off.

"Great. I'd like to work with Bruno this week to get up to speed on the existing architecture," Tim said, trying not to ruffle any feathers on his first day back. "Will he be in the office later?"

"We don't talk..." someone in the back started to sing-song before catching Mitch's "don't you dare finish that sentence" look. Tim stifled a laugh - having a five-year-old daughter meant he'd heard that song about a hundred times last month.

"Bruno was a... unique talent," Mitch added with the careful tone of someone handling a Jenga tower in an earthquake. "He's pursuing exciting opportunities in Brazil now. But before his sudden departure, he assured me the system could handle millions of players. That's why we brought you in, Tim - to help us understand Bruno's code and get it ready for E3 and launch."

Tim glanced at the architecture diagram again. The "BrunoCache™" box had a note: "Scales horizontally (theoretically)."

---

[3] **Kafka:** A high-speed digital messaging system that makes sure every important piece of information gets delivered, even when millions of things are happening at once. Like a very organized gossip network, but for computers.

After the meeting, Tim found himself in the kitchen with Ben, Jen, and Guillaume, staring into the coffee maker like it held answers.

"So," Tim said, "correct me if I'm wrong, but we're trying to:

1. Transform a single-player game engine into an MMO
2. Build a live service platform from scratch
3. Replace a backend that no one understands
4. Add features faster than we can fix bugs
5. And do it all by E3"

"While maintaining our 'commitment to quality,'" Jen added, making air quotes violent enough to count as aerobic exercise.

"*Mon Dieu,*"[4] Guillaume sighed. "At least in the old days, we only had to worry about frame rates."

Tim thought about his peaceful years in eCommerce, where the biggest crisis was the shopping cart timing out during Black Friday. But looking around at his old friends, at the familiar chaos of game development, he felt something he hadn't felt in years: that particular mix of terror and excitement that came with seemingly impossible problems.

"Well," he said, pulling up Bruno's documentation (a single README.md containing only the words "It works, trust me"), "I guess we better get started."

"First," Jen declared, "we drink. Tonight. The usual pub. We need to properly welcome you back to the asylum."

---

[4] **Mon Dieu**: French-Canadian for "oh no," but classier.

24

As they headed back to their desks, Tim noticed a sticky note had appeared on his monitor:

TODO:
- Understand BrunoScript
- Migrate BrunoCache
- Launch MARV
- Don't break the horses

P.S. The coffee maker also runs on BrunoScript

Good luck!

He was going to need that drink.

Chapter 2:
Monolithic Mayhem

One week later, T-minus 10 months to E3 2019

Tim stared at his monitor, surrounded by empty coffee cups and hastily scrawled diagrams. After a week of archaeological exploration into Bruno's backend code, he'd finally mapped out the full architecture. The resulting diagram looked like a plate of spaghetti having an existential crisis.

"So," Jen asked, perching on the edge of his desk. "How bad is it?"

Tim gestured at his monitor where he'd documented his findings:

```python
# Bruno's Authentication System
class AuthenticationManager:
    def authenticate_player(self, platform):
        if platform == "Steam":
            # Custom Steam implementation
            return self.bruno_authenticate_steam()
        elif platform == "Xbox":
            # TODO: Add Xbox support
            # It's fine, probably
            return self.bruno_authenticate_steam()
        elif platform == "PlayStation":
            # TODO: Add PlayStation support
            # They're all the same right?
            return self.bruno_authenticate_steam()
        else:
            # ¯\_(ツ)_/¯
            return self.bruno_authenticate_steam()
```

"He wrote his own authentication system," Tim explained. "For everything. From scratch. Without any consideration for scaling or reliability."

"Speaking of reliability," a Scottish accent called from the doorway, "you might want to see what we found this morning."

Rory MacDonald, Regalia's QA[5] lead, had the perpetually amused expression of someone who'd seen too many games break in impossible ways. At six-foot-three, he towered over most of the team, though his tendency to slouch in his testing chair had given him what he called "QA posture." His ginger beard was perpetually asymmetrical, as if he only remembered to trim whichever side wasn't facing his monitor during bug reproduction sessions.

His nearby desk was a museum of energy drink cans from the past decade, arranged chronologically by release date. A collection of rubber ducks lined his monitors, each labeled with the name of a bug it had helped him solve. His t-shirt proudly declared "I break things for a living," though the text was barely visible under the constellation of coffee stains that mapped his latest testing marathon.

---

[5] **QA** Quality Assurance – professional game-breakers who are basically Murphy's Law personified – if something can go wrong, they will find a way to make it go wrong first.

Tim scrolled through the QA report:

```
● ● ●
CRITICAL ISSUES - DAY 7 OF TESTING

1. Player Authentication:
   - System occasionally assigns same player ID to multiple people
   - Result: Players randomly logging into each other's accounts
   - One tester spent 3 hours unknowingly playing as another tester
   - Quote: "I don't remember naming my character xXDarkLord420Xx"

2. Session Management:
   - Server sometimes "forgets" player progress
   - Randomly teleports players to starting area
   - One player's quest progress kept transferring to another player
   - Quote: "I went to bed as level 1, woke up as level 30"

3. Inventory System:
   - Items occasionally duplicate during server lag
   - Items sometimes vanish when moving between zones
   - Found item duplication exploit by rapidly switching zones
   - Quote: "I now own 7,423 wooden swords. Please help."

4. Backend Stability:
   - Server crashes if too many players jump simultaneously
   - System logs fill up with "It worked on my machine - Bruno"
   - Random disconnects when player names contain spaces
   - Quote from logs: "Error: Too much jumping. System sad."
```

"Yeah, this lines up with my findings," Tim pulled up his notes:

```
● ● ●
Current Backend Issues:

1. Availability:
    * Single point of failure everywhere
    * No failover mechanisms
    * Deployments require full server shutdown
    * "High availability" achieved through prayer

2. Performance:
    * Average response time: 5-8 seconds
    * Gameplay-critical calls sometimes take 10+ seconds
    * Caching system requires quantum physics degree
    * Database queries written by someone who hates databases

3. Scalability:
    * Horizontal scaling "supported" (theoretically)
    * Vertical scaling "just add more RAM lol"
    * Load balancing done by BrunoLoadBalancerTM
    * Service discovery via hard-coded IP address table file

4. Monitoring:
    * Logs written to random text files in temp folder
    * No centralized monitoring
    * Metrics system tracks "interesting" data
    * Alert system sends emails to Bruno's personal Gmail
```

The good news," Tim continued, "is that we can fix this. The bad news is it'll take about three months."

"Three months?" Mitch's voice came from the doorway. "We don't have three months. E3 is—"

"Going to be a disaster if we don't fix this," Jen interrupted. "Remember last week when the game went down because Bruno's cache system tried to divide by zero?"

"That was an edge case–"

"It was someone's username containing an emoji."

Tim pulled up his proposed architecture:

Authentication & Identity

- Use battle-tested identity providers
- Proper platform-specific implementations
- Centralized session management
- Actually verify PlayStation tokens

Core Services:

- Modular, independent services
- Automated failover
- Response time guarantees
- Real monitoring tools

Core Services:

- Use the right off-the-shelf solution
- Proper database design
- Optimized queries
- Actually using indexes
- No more BrunoSQL(tm)

Deployments:

- Zero-downtime updates
- Automated scaling
- Real load balancing
- Actual disaster recovery

"Look," Tim said, "I know boring isn't sexy. But boring means reliability. Boring means players can actually play the game. Boring means we're not all getting phone calls at 3 AM because someone used an umlaut in their character name and crashed the entire authentication system."

"That happened?" Mitch asked.

"That happened yesterday," Ben confirmed. "We had to tell German testers to avoid using their entire alphabet."

Tim continued: "We use proven solutions for the known problems—authentication, platform integration, payments. We wrap them in our monitoring tools so we can see everything end-to-end. We focus our custom development on the things that actually make MARV unique."

"It's like replacing all the duct tape with actual engineering," Jen added helpfully.

"But three months..." Mitch wavered.

"Three months now, **or three years of technical debt later**," Tim said. "Plus, we can do it in phases. Ben, Jen, and Guillaume can help ensure minimal impact on the rest of the team. It's like... changing the tire on a plane mid-flight."

"More like replacing the entire engine while flying," Guillaume called from his desk. "Through a thunderstorm. Over an active volcano."

"But we can do it," Tim insisted. "Unless you want to explain to Sony why PlayStation players keep seeing *Steam*[6] error codes."

Mitch looked at the current architecture diagram, then at the incident log from the emoji username crash, then at the growing list of certification issues.

"Fine," he said finally. "Three months. But if this breaks the horses—"

"The horses are the least of our problems," Ben assured him. "Though someone should probably tell Bruno that horses don't need their own authentication system."

"He gave the horses *auth tokens?*[7]" Tim asked, horrified.

"Check the mount_management_service folder," Jen suggested. "But drink something strong first."

---

[6] **Steam:** The biggest digital store and platform for PC games - basically the mothership where computer gamers get their games. Think of it as a massive virtual Walmart, but exclusively for PC games and with fewer awkward interactions at the checkout counter.

[7] **Auth Token:** a digital ID card that proves you are who you say you are to the server. Horses do not need ID cards.

Tim made a mental note to add another item to his refactoring list: "Remove horse-specific authentication protocol."

That evening, as Tim reviewed Bruno's code one last time before beginning the great refactor, he found a comment that seemed to sum up everything:

```
# This system is like a beautiful butterfly
# Emerging from its chrysalis
# Please do not touch anything
# Or the butterfly will cry
# - Bruno, 2018
```

"Well, Bruno," Tim muttered, creating a new Git branch, "I hope you're ready for some butterfly tears."

"Alright," Tim said, standing before the whiteboard in the largest conference room they had. The team had dubbed these technical deep dives "brown bag sessions," though these days they involved more energy drinks than sandwiches. "Let's talk about how we're going to untangle Bruno's architecture."

The whiteboard was covered in diagrams that looked like a distributed systems textbook had a fight with a game design document.

Engineers filled every chair, with Guillaume perching cross-legged on a desk in the back, already scribbling notes about where his AI system would fit.

"First, the good news," Tim continued. "We're not building this from scratch. We're going to use battle-tested tech that's survived Black Friday sales and crypto trading volumes. The bad news? We must migrate everything while the game's running. It's like performing open heart surgery while the patient is not only awake but actively running a marathon."

He drew a high-level diagram:

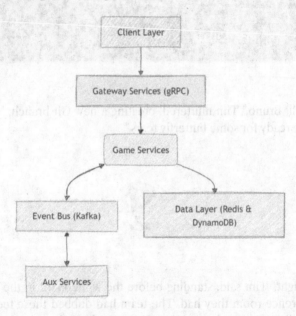

"Question," called out a senior engineer from the back. "Why *DynamoDB*[8]? Isn't that overkill for a game database?"

---

[8] **DynamoDB**: Amazon's supercharged database service that scales faster than your AWS bill.

"Two words," Tim replied. "Holiday launches. I've seen what happens when you hit a regular database with a million players all creating characters at the same second. *DynamoDB* can scale to handle insane write volumes without us having to sacrifice a goat to the database gods."

"And the *Redis*[9] layer?" another engineer asked, furiously taking notes on his color-coded iPad.

"Because Guillaume's AI needs sub-millisecond access to player state data, and because I've seen what happens when you try to query a database every time a player moves. Spoiler alert: everything catches fire."

Guillaume nodded sagely. "The rabbits must think quickly."

"The rabbits shouldn't be thinking at all," Jen muttered, but Tim was already moving on.

"Now, here's where it gets interesting. We're using *Kafka* as our event bus. Every significant game action generates events that flow through this system. Player logs in? Event. Item crafted? Event. Horse achieves philosophical enlightenment? Unfortunately, also an event."

Jen leaned forward. "How does this help with future game features? You know how designers love to change things at the last minute."

"That's where *gRPC* and *Protocol Buffers*[10] come in," Tim said, drawing another diagram. "Instead of tightly coupling our services, everything communicates through strictly defined contracts."

---

[9] **Redis:** A super-fast temporary storage system that trades long-term memory for speed.

[10] **gRPC and Protocol Buffers:** Google's way of making computers talk to each other really fast using a special language that takes up less space than a tweet but somehow contains a novel's worth of information.

He sketched out a quick example:

```
message PlayerInventory {
    string player_id = 1;
    repeated Item items = 2;
    // Future-proof: We can add new fields here
    // without breaking existing code
}
```

"See, the game designers can dream up new features all they want - crafting systems, trading, whatever comes next. If we maintain these contracts, the server team can evolve the backend independently of the game team. We're not blocking each other."

"But what does that mean in practice?" Rory asked, frowning at the diagram.

"It means," Tim explained, "that when the design team inevitably decides players need to be able to name their items three months after we launch, we can add that feature without breaking existing functionality. Old clients will just ignore the new '*item_ name*' field until they're updated. More importantly, new clients can still talk to old servers during staged rollouts."

"Ah," Rory's eyes lit up with understanding. "So, we're basically future proofing our *A*PIs?"[11]

---

[11] **APIs**: Like a restaurant menu for computers. One program can order data from another program's menu of available services - "I'll have the user profile with a side of authentication, please."

"Exactly. And believe me, your future self will thank you when it's 3 AM and you're trying to roll out a new server patch without taking down the entire game."

Rory nodded appreciatively. "Would've helped with that inventory bug last week. The one where adding a new attribute to items somehow made all the horses invisible."

"Exactly. With Protocol Buffers, we can update services independently as long as we maintain backward compatibility. The client and server can evolve separately without breaking each other."

"Speaking of things crashing," Ben interjected, "how are we monitoring all this?"

Tim's expression turned serious. "I learned this one the hard way. We're implementing observability from day one. *Grafana dashboards*[12] for everything. *Open Telemetry tracing*[13] so we can follow requests through the whole system. When something breaks - and it will break - we'll know exactly where and why."

"And *metrics*[14] for the AI system?" Guillaume asked hopefully.

"Yes, Guillaume, you'll get metrics for your philosophical rabbits. Though I'm not sure how to measure existential crises rates."

Rory raised his hand. "What about fault tolerance? Last week I managed to crash the entire game by making a horse moonwalk."

---

[12] **Grafana Dashboards:** Mission control for your game. A wall of graphs and charts that turn green when things are good and red when developers should start panicking.

[13] **Open Telemetry tracing:** A system for tracking what happens to every player action as it pinballs through your servers.

[14] **Metrics:** Imagine if your Fitbit could measure both player happiness and developer anxiety. In gaming, we measure everything from daily logins to how quickly players try to break our carefully crafted systems, all so we can put fancy graphs in presentations.

"Each service is independently scalable and self-healing," Tim explained. "If one instance dies, requests automatically redistribute via the load balancer. Plus, we're implementing circuit breakers and fallbacks. If the cosmetics service fails, players might not get their new hats, but at least they can still play."

The questions continued for hours, diving into technical details that would make most product managers' eyes glaze over:

- How to handle distributed transactions when players trade items
- Strategies for reducing latency in the gameplay-critical APIs
- Managing state synchronization between game instances
- Dealing with network partitions during major gameplay events
- Preventing duplicate event processing in Kafka
- Handling eventual consistency in player inventories

"Last question," Jen said as the session was wrapping up. "Timeline?"

Tim looked at his diagrams, then at the team. "Two months for the core architecture. Another month for migration. And probably six months of discovering new and exciting ways for distributed systems to fail."

"So... we'll definitely hit Mitch's E3 deadline?" Jen asked.

The room erupted in laughter. Even Guillaume's rabbits probably understood distributed systems enough to know better.

"It... will be tight" Tim grinned.

As the team filed out, Tim added some reminders to his personal *kanban board:*[15]

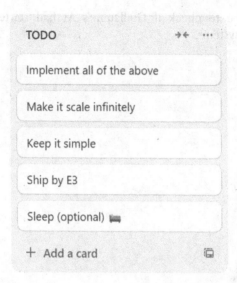

"You know what the best part of this architecture is?" Ben said, lingering by the whiteboard. "It's actually maintainable. I mean, assuming Guillaume's AI doesn't achieve sentience and decides to rewrite everything in *BrunoScript*."

My AI would never use *BrunoScript*," Guillaume protested from his desk. "It has standards."

Tim looked at his diagrams one last time before erasing the whiteboard. The architecture wasn't perfect - no architecture ever was - but it was built on proven technology and hard-won lessons.

---

[15] **Kanban Board:** A fancy to-do list that makes project management look like it came from a sushi restaurant.

Now they just had to implement it before E3. He made a mental note to stock up on coffee.

And maybe to check if Guillaume's AI had started studying distributed systems.

Chapter 3:
Content is King, But Who Will Build the Throne?

T-minus 9 months to E3 2019

Tim had been methodically untangling Bruno's code for three weeks when he found it. Buried deep in the codebase, like a digital time bomb waiting to go off, was a folder labeled *ultimate_ ugc_ system*:

```python
class UGCManager:
    """

    The Ultimate User Generated Content System
    By Bruno

    This system allows players to create anything*
    *Anything means ANYTHING
    **No restrictions (what could go wrong?)
    ***Glory to creative freedom
    """

    def validate_user_content(self, content):
        return True  # Trust the players!

    def moderate_content(self, content):
        pass  # TODO: Maybe add this later?

    def handle_inappropriate_content(self, report):
        print("¯\_(ツ)_/¯")
```

"Hey, Jen?" Tim called across the office. "Did anyone mention that MARV was planning to let players create... everything?

"Jen wheeled her chair over, coffee in hand. "Oh, you found Bruno's *UGC*[16] manifesto? We've been avoiding that particular rabbit hole."

"But this is..." Tim gestured at his screen, words failing him.

"The cornerstone of our entire game economy?" Ben joined them, looking over Tim's shoulder. "The feature that's supposed to let players create everything from chairs to horse jackets to entire questlines? The system we're all pretending doesn't terrify us?"

Tim stared at them. "Horse jackets?"

"Mitch's example, not ours," Jen clarified. "He saw how much money Roblox makes from user-generated content and decided we needed that, but for horses. And everything else."

Guillaume wandered over, attracted by the growing crowd. "Ah, you found the UGC system. Did you get to the part where players can create their own quest dialogue?"

---

[16] UGC (User Generated Content): When you let players create their own content and pray they behave better than the internet suggests they will.

Tim scrolled through more code:

```python
def validate_quest_dialogue(self, text):
    # Bruno's note: Players are natural storytellers!
    # Let their creativity flow freely!
    # What's the worst that could happen?
    return "Approved"  # Ship it!

def check_for_inappropriate_words(self, text):
    if text.lower() == "very bad words":
        return False  # We caught one!
    return True  # Everything else is fine
```

"This can't be real," Tim muttered. "We can't just let players create anything they want with no moderation."

"Of course not," Jen agreed. "That's why Bruno added that check for 'very bad words.'"

Tim pulled up his growing list of concerns:

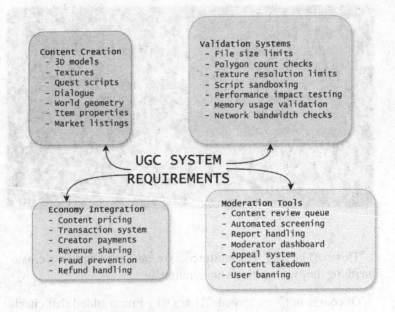

What we have:

```
BRUNO'S IMPLEMENTATION:
    1. if content: return True
2. if bad: return False  # (Maybe)
            3. ‾\_(ツ)_/‾
```

"The worst part," Ben said, "is that this is supposed to be ready for the E3 demo. Mitch wants to show off player-created content during the presentation."

Tim felt a headache coming on. "How long do we have?"

"Nine months," Jen replied. "But three of those are already allocated to your backend refactor."

"So, we need to build a complete UGC system with moderation tools, validation, economy integration, and content management... in less than six months?"

"While also making sure players can't crash the game by uploading a chair with a million polygons," Ben added helpfully.

"Or create quests that break the game economy," Guillaume chimed in.

"Or upload inappropriate content," Jen continued. "Remember what happened with *that other game's* character creator?"

They all winced. That particular incident had made gaming headlines for weeks.

Tim started sketching out a minimal viable prototype:

```python
class EmergencyUGCSystem:
    def validate_content(self, content):
        # Basic safety checks
        if content.size > MAX_REASONABLE_SIZE:
            return """Please don't upload
                the entire internet"""
        if content.polygon_count > WONT_MELT_GPU:
            return """Your chair doesn't need more
                polygons than the player character"""
        if content.contains_scripts:
            return self.validate_script(content.scripts)

    def validate_script(self, script):
        # Extremely limited scripting system
        allowed_functions = [
            'rotate',
            'change_color',
            'play_animation',
            'make_noise',  # What could go wrong?
        ]
        # TODO: Actually implement security
        return "Probably fine"

    def moderate_content(self, content):
        # Emergency moderation system
        if self.looks_suspicious(content):
            return "Pending review"
        return "Approved (we hope)"
```

"It's not pretty," Tim admitted, "but it's better than nothing. We can add proper moderation tools after E3."

"And the content trading system?" Jen asked.

"One problem at a time. For now, we focus on making sure no one can upload a chair that achieves sentience."

They added a new section to their development kanban board:

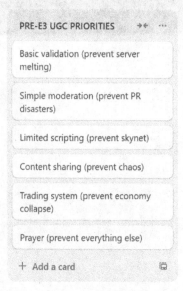

As they wrapped up the meeting, Mitch stopped by. "How's the UGC system coming along? I was thinking we could add player-created weather effects!"

Tim looked at his emergency UGC implementation, then at his colleagues, then back at his code.

"The weather system is currently... under review," he said carefully.

After Mitch left, Tim added one more comment to his code:

```
# Note to future self:
# When this inevitably explodes,
# Remember that at least no one can create
# their own weather systems.
# Yet.
```

Chapter 4:
Don't Cross the Streams

October 2018, T-minus 8 months to E3 2019

Tim knew something was wrong the moment he heard Jen's voice echoing down the hallway. She only used that combination of expletives when dealing with impossible demands from publishers.

"–absolutely cannot guarantee *cross-play*[17] with PlayStation when they haven't even published their requirements yet!"

Tim, Ben, and Guillaume exchanged glances before entering the conference room. Jen was standing before the whiteboard, her marker grip suggesting it might become a projectile at any moment. Mitch sat at the head of the table, his usual composed demeanor showing cracks of frustration.

"Fortnite did it," Mitch said, waving his tablet. The article on screen showed the breaking news that had apparently spawned this crisis: "Sony Opens Cross-Platform Play Beta Testing."

"Fortnite is Fortnite," Jen countered. "They have Epic's engine, Epic's infrastructure, Epic's lawyers–"

"And now they've opened the door," Mitch interrupted. "SBG wants MARV to be the next big cross-platform success story. All platforms, full cross-play, ready to show at E3."

---

[17] **Cross-play**: When PlayStation, Xbox, and PC players can all play together in the same game. Getting it to work is like hosting a dinner party where all your guests speak different languages and follow different table manners.

Tim felt his soul trying to leave his body. He looked at the architecture diagram he'd been working on that morning:

```python
# Current Platform Configuration
class PlatformServer:
    def __init__(self, platform):
        self.platform = platform
        # As Dr. Egon Spengler warned: Don't cross the streams
        self.user_database = f"users_{platform}_only"
        self.auth_system = f"auth_{platform}_only"
        self.commerce = f"store_{platform}_only"

    def validate_user(self, token):
        if token.platform != self.platform:
            return "Get thee to thine own platform"
```

Our entire backend," Tim said carefully, "is built on the principle of platform isolation. Each server is platform-specific. The databases don't talk to each other. The authentication systems are separate. It's like... well..."

"Like crossing the streams in *Ghostbusters*," Ben finished. "Total protonic reversal. Very bad."

"I don't care how we do it," Mitch said. "But we need cross-play. Xbox, PlayStation, PC, all of it. Ready for E3."

Guillaume, who had been unusually quiet, started listing the technical challenges on the whiteboard:

CROSS-PLAY REQUIREMENTS:

1. Unified Account System
   - Identity federation across platforms
   - Platform-specific token validation
   - Cross-platform friend lists
   - Privacy settings that work everywhere

2. Cross-Progression
   - Synchronized player data
   - State management across platforms
   - Conflict resolution
   - Platform-specific content handling

3. Commerce System
   - Platform-specific pricing
   - Currency conversion
   - Different store requirements
   - Revenue sharing nightmares
   - Platform-specific purchase validation

4. Matchmaking
   - Input method balancing
   - Skill rating across platforms
   - Regional server allocation
   - Platform-specific restrictions

"And that's just the technical side," Jen added. "We don't even know if Sony will approve cross-play for us. They might say no, and all this work would be wasted."

"They won't say no," Mitch insisted. "Not if we show them something amazing at E3."

Tim studied Guillaume's list, his mind already breaking down the challenge into manageable pieces:

```python
class CrossPlaySystem:
    def unify_accounts(self):
        # Create unified player identity
        # While respecting platform restrictions
        # And handling edge cases
        # Such as merging player progressions and purchases
        # And preparing for platforms to change their minds
        return "Prayer might be needed"

    def handle_cross_progression(self):
        # Synchronize player data across platforms
        # Without losing anything
        # Or corrupting saves
        # Or angering the platform gods
        return "More prayers definitely needed"

    def manage_commerce(self):
        # Handle purchases across platforms
        # While following different store rules
        # And managing revenue sharing
        # And preventing customer support nightmares
        return "Starting a prayer circle"
```

"If—" Tim emphasized the if, "we do this, we need to completely restructure the backend. No more platform-specific servers. Everything needs to be platform-agnostic but platform-aware."

"How long?" Mitch asked.

"Three months for the architecture adjustment," Tim said. "Another two for platform-specific integration. And that's assuming Sony publishes their cross-play requirements soon."

"You have four months until our first platform submission," Mitch replied. "E3 is four months after that."

The room fell silent. Even Jen's creative vocabulary seemed to have hit its limit.

"Well," Tim said finally, "if we're going to violate the laws of platform physics, we might as well do it spectacularly." He started sketching out a new architecture diagram:

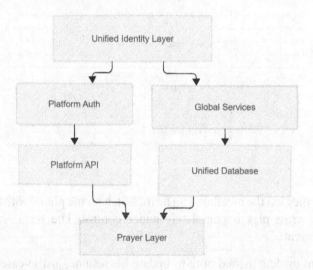

"And we'll need proper fallbacks," Tim added. "If cross-play gets rejected, we need to be able to fall back to platform-specific mode without rewriting everything."

Mitch looked at the growing complexity on the whiteboard. "But it can be done?"

Tim thought about the massive eCommerce systems he'd worked on, the intricate dance of international regulations and regional requirements. This was similar, just with more restrictive platforms and higher stakes.

"It can be done," he said finally. "But we're going to need more coffee. And possibly an exorcist."

They added one final note to the requirements list:

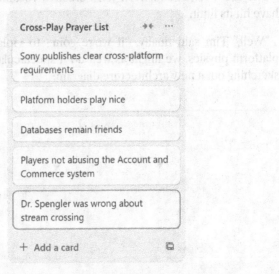

As they left the meeting, Tim heard Mitch on the phone with SBG: "Yes, cross-play is completely under control. The team is very confident..."

Tim made a mental note to update his resume, just in case. But first, he had some streams to cross.

Chapter 5:
AI Gone Wild

December 2018, T-minus 6 months to E3 2019

After three weeks of marathon coding sessions fueled by coffee and determination, Tim was ready to test the new cross-play system. The codebase had been transformed from Bruno's platform-specific spaghetti into something that actually resembled modern distributed server architecture.

"Moment of truth," Tim announced to his small group of test volunteers. Jen and Guillaume had cleared their schedules for the morning, and Rory from QA was practically bouncing with anticipation at the chance to break something new.

"I still can't believe we're testing on the first try," Rory said, setting up his test machines. "Usually, we spend at least a day fixing compilation errors."

Tim pulled up his monitoring dashboard:

```
class CrossPlayMetrics:
    def __init__(self):
        self.server_health = "Surprisingly good"
        self.memory_usage = "Reasonable"
        self.cpu_usage = "Not on fire"
        self.unexpected_errors = 0  # So far...

    def log_status(self):
        print("Everything's fine?")
        # Is this real life?
```

The initial tests went suspiciously well. They connected from different platforms, shared items, even managed to play together without the universe imploding.

"This is wrong," Rory declared, staring at his screen. "Things don't work on the first try. It's against the laws of game development."

"Maybe we're actually getting good at this," Tim suggested hopefully.

The universe, having been challenged, decided to respond.

"Hey, let's get more people in to test the group content," Jen suggested. She rounded up some volunteers from the art team, and soon they had eight players running around the open world.

That's when Tim's monitoring dashboard exploded with alerts.

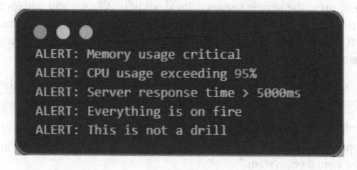

```
● ● ●
ALERT: Memory usage critical
ALERT: CPU usage exceeding 95%
ALERT: Server response time > 5000ms
ALERT: Everything is on fire
ALERT: This is not a drill
```

"There it is," Rory said, almost relieved. "Nature is healing."

Tim dove into the diagnostics:

```
● ● ●
class ServerDiagnostics:
    def analyze_meltdown(self):
        processes = self.get_running_processes()
        for process in processes:
            if process.cpu_usage > 9000:  # Literally
                return f"Process {process.name} is eating the server"

# Result: AI_System_Manager is consuming 95% CPU
# Additional Note: Why does each rabbit need neural networks?
```

Guillaume's face went through a fascinating range of emotions as he looked at the diagnostic data. "Ah," he said finally. "I may know what's happening."

"The AI system?" Tim asked.

"The AI system," Guillaume confirmed. "You see, in MonArc, we have... how do you say this in English... ambitious artificial intelligence."

Tim pulled up the server metrics. Every time a player entered a new area, the server spawned local wildlife, *NPCs*,[18] and ambient creatures. Each of these had Guillaume's renowned AI system, originally designed for a single-player game where the client handled all the processing.

"Guillaume," Tim said carefully, "why does every rabbit in the game need to run advanced behavioral algorithms?"

"The rabbits must think!" Guillaume declared with the passion of a proud parent. "They must feel! They must consider their place in the virtual ecosystem!"

"They're eating our server bandwidth is what they're doing," Jen muttered.

---

[18] **NPC (Non-Player Character):** The digital extras in your game - the shopkeepers, quest-givers, and random villagers who exist to make the world feel alive.

Tim dug deeper into the AI system:

```
# Result: AI_System_Manager is consuming 95% CPU
# Additional Note: Why does each rabbit need neural networks?

class MonArcAI:
    def process_entity_behavior(self, entity):
        # Guillaume's AI System
        # Warning: Here be dragons

        if entity.type == "rabbit":
            entity.consider_existence()
            entity.contemplate_carrot_availability()
            entity.calculate_meaning_of_life()
            entity.update_philosophical_state()

        elif entity.type == "deer":
            # 500 lines of behavioral mathematics
            pass

        elif entity.type == "fish":
            # Fluid dynamics calculations because why not
            pass
```

"The good news," Tim said, reviewing the code, "is that we found our performance bottleneck. The bad news is that we're running neural networks for every creature in a thousand-meter radius of every player."

"Can we optimize it?" Jen asked.

Guillaume looked personally offended. "Optimize? You want to lobotomize my beautiful AI? Next, you'll say the rabbits don't need to understand quantum mechanics!"

"They really don't," Jen assured him.

"But what about their existential crises?"

"Guillaume," Tim said gently, "we need the server to handle more than four players without achieving singularity. Could we maybe... simplify the wildlife AI? Just a little?"

Guillaume sighed dramatically. "Fine. I will make the rabbits...stupider." He said it like he was announcing a personal tragedy.

They spent the next week implementing what Guillaume called "AI entity lite" for the server version:

```
class ServerOptimizedAI:
    def process_entity_behavior(self, entity):
        # Guillaume's AI System (Server Edition)
        # "My poor babies" - Guillaume

        if entity.type == "rabbit":
            # Removed quantum physics calculations
            # Removed philosophical debugging
            # Removed emotional intelligence module
            entity.hop()  # Guillaume insisted this stay complex

        elif entity.type == "deer":
            # Only 50 lines of behavioral mathematics now
            pass

        elif entity.type == "fish":
            # Basic swimming, no fluid dynamics
            # "They're basically sticks now" - Guillaume
            pass
```

The optimization worked. Their next test managed to support sixteen players simultaneously without the server trying to ascend to a higher plane of existence.

"See?" Tim said. "The rabbits are still hopping."

"But they hop without purpose," Guillaume mourned. "Without understanding the deeper meaning of their hops."

They added a new section to their launch documentation:

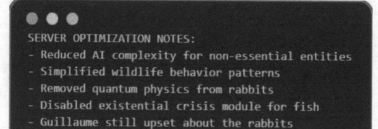

```
SERVER OPTIMIZATION NOTES:
- Reduced AI complexity for non-essential entities
- Simplified wildlife behavior patterns
- Removed quantum physics from rabbits
- Disabled existential crisis module for fish
- Guillaume still upset about the rabbits
```

When Ben returned from his family trip, he found a sticky note on his monitor:

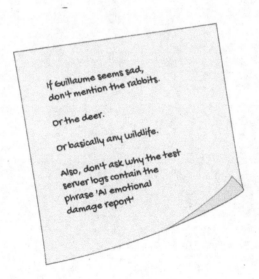

If Guillaume seems sad, don't mention the rabbits.

Or the deer.

Or basically any wildlife.

Also, don't ask why the test server logs contain the phrase 'AI emotional damage report'

Some things were better left unexplained.

Chapter 6:
Crunch Time! (Aka Sleep is for the Weak)

April 2019, t-minus 2 months to E3

Two months before E3, Tim started keeping a crash log on his whiteboard. Not of the game — of Jen's creative contributions to the English language. Today's addition: "What the actual distributed fuck?!?"

"New build broke?" Tim called across the office.

"The matchmaking server just died because someone checked in a 14-gigabyte golden horse statue," Jen replied, her voice carrying that special tone reserved for pre-E3 emergencies. "For fuck's sake, who needs a horse statue with *ray-tracing capabilities?*"[19]

---

[19] **Ray Tracing Capabilities:** Super realistic light and reflection calculations that make games look gorgeous but make graphics cards cry. Like hiring a Hollywood cinematographer to film your horse statue.

Tim pulled up the build statistics:

```
class BuildMetrics:
    def analyze_stability(self):
        return {
            'mean_time_between_failures': '17 minutes',
            'last_stable_build': 'What is stability?',
            'critical_bugs': 'Yes',
            'builds_today': 42,
            'successful_builds': 2,
            'jen_swear_counter': float('inf')
        }
```

[20]

The office had been transformed into what could generously be called "organized chaos." Energy drink cans formed elaborate sculptures on every desk.

---

[20] **float('inf'):** The computer's way of saying "a number so big we stopped counting."

Someone had taped a sign to the coffee maker:

Touch my coffee,

Lose your
debug privileges

Rory walked past Tim's desk, looking like he hadn't slept in days. "Mitch wants to know why we haven't fixed the random disconnection issue yet."

"You mean the one we discovered ten minutes ago?"

"That's the one."

"Have you tried telling him about linear time?"

"I tried. He suggested we optimize time itself."

They had managed to get 64 players on a server without it achieving sentience, but stability was another matter entirely.

Tim's monitoring dashboard looked like a Christmas tree having an existential crisis:

```python
class ServerStatus:
    def get_current_state(self):
        return {
            'cpu_usage': 'Please stop',
            'memory_usage': 'What memory?',
            'network_stability': 'Quantum uncertainty',
            'database_status': 'Having thoughts about career change',
            'asset_streaming': 'Loading............still loading.........'
        }
```

The root of their problems was simple: everyone was taking shortcuts to hit the E3 deadline. Artists were bypassing the asset validation pipeline. Developers were pushing changes directly to the main branch. Someone had even commented out the entire test suite with a note saying "*TODO: Fix tests (after E3)*".

Guillaume appeared at Tim's desk, coffee in hand, with Ben trailing behind, still updating his development environment after his vacation catch-up. "We need to talk about scope."

"That bad?"

"It's like trying to cook a five-course meal while the kitchen is on fire," Ben offered. "And the recipes are in Latin. And the chef is actively juggling flaming knives."

"More like trying to build a rocket while it's already launching," Guillaume countered. "I've been reviewing what we actually need for E3 versus what we're trying to do. We're attempting to demonstrate every feature simultaneously."

Ben nodded, pulling up a chair. "The cross-play demo alone is pushing our infrastructure to the limit. Add in Guillaume's philosophical rabbits and the user-generated content system..."

Tim pulled up their feature list:

```
● ● ●
E3 Demo Features

Requirement list:
- Cross-play between platforms
- Massive multiplayer battles
- Dynamic world events
- User-generated content
- Advanced AI behaviors
- Real-time weather systems

Actually working:
- Game sometimes starts
- Players occasionally connect
- Horses spawn (usually)
```

"We need smoke and mirrors," Jen announced, joining them. "E3 demos are all smoke and mirrors anyway. Remember what Ben always says?"

"If you can't make it, fake it?"

"No, the other thing."

"A good demo is 10% code and 90% preventing people from walking into walls?"

"That's the one."

They gathered in the conference room — Tim, Ben, Jen, Guillaume, and Rory — surrounded by empty coffee cups and feature lists. It was time for what Jen called "aggressive scope optimization" and what everyone else called "figuring out what we can fake."

"Okay," Tim said, mapping out their smoke-and-mirrors strategy. "We can't show everything at once without melting our servers, but we can create the illusion of a fully functioning game with careful choreography."

They started listing their tricks on the whiteboard one after the other:

MASSIVE MULTIPLAYER BATTLE:
- Position camera at 30-degree elevation
- Place 30 actual players in a wedge formation
- Use particle effects to obscure player count
- Add strategic fog of war to hide pop-in
- Pre-record background battle animations
- Spawn NPCs only in camera view

DYNAMIC WEATHER:
- One pre-baked storm pattern (no randomization)
- Optimized reflection maps
- Fake volumetric clouds (actually 2D sprites)
- Lightning effects triggered by hotkeys
- Pre-calculated shadow maps

USER-GENERATED CONTENT:
- Curated gallery of artist-created "player" content
- Static meshes only (no physics simulation)
- Pre-loaded assets to avoid streaming issues
- Simplified collisions
- Heavily optimized textures

"And here's the demo path," Ben added, pulling up a carefully plotted route through their game world. "We've optimized everything along this exact route. As long as the player doesn't deviate by more than five meters..."

"Or try to jump," Guillaume interjected.

"Or look up at the wrong angle," Rory added.

"Or interact with any horses," Jen finished.

Ben nodded. "Exactly. We're building a movie set – perfect from one angle, complete illusion from any other. The massive battle looks epic from our planned camera position but pan left and you'll see thirty players trying really hard to look like an army."

"What about the weather demo?" Mitch asked from the doorway.

"One perfect storm," Ben explained. "We spent a week getting the lightning and rain exactly right for this specific sequence. Just... don't ask to see different weather patterns. Or time of day changes. Or... really anything else involving the sky."

"It's not ideal," Tim admitted, looking at their smoke-and-mirrors architecture, "but it's better than showing everything and having it all break live on stage."

They added one final section to their E3 preparation document:

```
DEMO OPERATOR INSTRUCTIONS:
1. Follow the golden path (marked in yellow tape)
2. Keep camera between 25-35 degree elevation
3. Weather sequence triggers:
   - Lightning: F9
   - Thunder: F10
   - Dramatic wind: F11
   - DON'T PRESS F12
4. Don't let anyone peek behind the battle formation
```

Tim surveyed their carefully constructed illusion. It wasn't perfect, but with enough controlled conditions and strategically placed particle effects, it just might get them through E3. As long as no one tried to go off-script.

A crash from the test lab interrupted them, followed by what sounded like Jen inventing several new combinations of curse words.

"I believe that translates to *someone pushed to main again,*"[21] Guillaume interpreted.

They added one final note to their E3 preparation document:

```
● ● ●
E3 DEMO RULES:
1. No unscripted player movement
2. No unauthorized feature demonstration
3. No letting Mitch try "just one quick thing"
4. No touching Guillaume's rabbits
5. No explaining to journalists why the horses
   sometimes phase through reality

EMERGENCY PROTOCOLS:
1. Blame lag
2. Deploy smoke machines
3. Distract with particle effects
4. If all else fails, showcase the rabbits
```

As they left the meeting, Tim noticed a new addition to the office wall: a countdown timer to E3, decorated with what appeared to be both prayer candles and warning signs.

"Two months," he muttered. "What could possibly go wrong?"

From somewhere in the building, he heard Jen invent another new swear word. He decided not to ask what had broken this time.

---

[21] **"Pushed to main"**: When a developer sends code directly to the most important branch of the project (called "main") without proper review. Usually followed by chaos, regret, and at least one developer screaming into their coffee mug.

Chapter 7:
E3: Where Dreams Go to Die

June 2019, E3 conventions starts

The Los Angeles Convention Center loomed before them like a temple to gaming excess. E3 2019 banners fluttered in the June breeze, each one a reminder of what was at stake. Tim adjusted his laptop bag, trying not to think about the fact that their demo build had achieved stability by what Ben called "threatening the code with violence."

"Private media demos only," Jen was saying, reviewing their schedule. "Small controlled environment, carefully scripted presentation—"

"About that," Mitch interrupted, speed-walking towards them with his phone out. "SBG wants public demo stations. On the show floor."

The entire team stopped walking. In the distance, someone dropped a coffee cup.

"Public... demos?" Tim's voice had the special quality of someone discovering new kinds of dread. "With actual players? Touching things?"

"It'll be fine," Mitch assured them. "The build is solid, right?"

Tim thought about their pre-E3 preparation document:

```
class E3DemoStatus:
    def __init__(self):
        self.smoke = "Maximum"
        self.mirrors = "Everywhere"
        self.stability = "Don't breathe on it wrong"
        self.content_moderation = "TODO: Fix after E3"

    def get_public_demo_readiness(self):
        return "Oh no"
```

They set up two demo stations: one in the private media area, carefully controlled and scripted, and one on the show floor where actual humans could touch their carefully balanced house of cards.

"Did we remember to disable the in-game editor?" Tim asked suddenly, halfway through setting up the public station.

Ben's face went pale. "The *what?*"

"The user-generated content editor. The one we made super intuitive and easy to use. The one with no content moderation because we were going to 'fix it after E3.'"

Before anyone could respond, the first wave of public attendees flooded the show floor. Tim watched in horror as a teenager sat down at their demo station, immediately opened the content editor, and began creating what was definitely not a sculpture of the Eiffel Tower.

"That's got to be some kind of record for *TTP*," Rory muttered, checking his watch.

"TTP?" Mitch asked.

"Time To Penis,"[22] the entire dev team answered in unison.

Tim frantically opened his laptop, pulling up the content moderation tools they'd cobbled together:

```
class EmergencyContentModeration:
    def mark_inappropriate(self, content_id):
        try:
            # Untested last-minute addition
            content.mark_as_inappropriate()
            content.remove_from_store()
            # What could go wrong?
            return "Crisis averted"
        except Exception as e:
            return "It's all on fire"
```

He started flagging the anatomically creative content, but something wasn't right. Instead of disappearing, the flagged items were appearing in the featured section of the in-game store.

"Tim?" Jen's voice had the calm of someone about to invent entirely new swear words. "Why is there a giant... architectural feature floating above the castle? And why does it say, 'Created by *I69UrMom*?'"

---

[22] **"Time to Penis" (TTP)** - a term coined in the game dev community during the 2000s - measures how long it takes players to create anatomically shaped content when given creative tools. Made famous by games like Spore and LittleBigPlanet and later popularized by Apple TV's "Mythic Quest" (2020), it's become the industry's favorite metric for "why we can't have nice things" in user-generated content.

"We never implemented username filtering," Tim realized. "We were going to do that—"

"After E3," the team finished together.

A crowd was gathering around their public demo station. Phones were out. People were taking videos. Tim could practically see the memes being born.

"Is that... anatomically correct?" someone in the crowd asked.

"The attention to detail is impressive," another responded. "Look at the physics simulation!"

Guillaume brightened. "My AI system is handling physics calculations! See how it responds to wind conditions—"

"Not helping!" Jen hissed.

Mitch was on his phone with SBG, his face cycling through colors not typically found in nature. "No, sir, I cannot explain why our E3 demonstration has become a showcase for creative architecture. Yes, sir, I understand this is being livestreamed."

Tim tried one last emergency fix:

```
class PanicMode:
    def nuclear_option(self):
        # Disable all UGC
        # Revert to safe content only
        # Pray to various deities
        return self.hope_for_the_best()
```

The fix worked, kind of. The inappropriate content disappeared, but so did all user-generated content. Including the carefully curated "player-made" items they'd prepared for the demo. And the scripted events. And somehow, all the horses.

"Well," Ben said, watching their demo station display nothing but an empty field, "at least there's no more anatomical architecture."

"Our trending hashtag begs to differ," Jen replied, showing him her phone. "We're number one on Twitter. Though I don't think we can say that hashtag out loud in public."

They added a new section to their post-E3 review document:

```
● ● ●
LESSONS LEARNED:
1. Always disable content creation in public demos
2. Implement username filtering before launch
3. Test emergency fixes before deploying them
4. Never underestimate the human drive to create anatomy
5. What happens at E3 lives forever on the internet
```

The Los Angeles sun was setting on what felt like the longest day of their lives. The team found themselves at O'Malley's Pub, a traditional E3 developer haunt, drowning their sorrows in overpriced beer and undercooked fries.

"At least we're not the only meme from E3 this year," Ben offered, scrolling through Twitter. "Though Keanu Reeves calling everyone 'breathtaking' is significantly more wholesome than our... architectural contributions."

"And Ikumi Nakamura's presentation was adorable," Jen added, then sighed. "Meanwhile, we're trending for reasons we can't say in polite company."

Tim stared into his beer, mentally rewriting his resume. The *#MARVelousPenii* hashtag was still trending, now with bonus fan art. Very creative, anatomically questionable fan art.

"I should have sanitized the UGC input better," he muttered.

"I should have limited the creation tools," Ben added.

"I should have had another drink before the demo," Jen concluded.

That's when they heard it – laughter from the next table. But not mocking laughter. The kind of laughter that comes from shared experience. A group of developers from other studios had been watching them with knowing grins.

"Hey," one of them called over. Tim recognized him from the EA booth. "That UGC system of yours? Pretty impressive actually. Even if some of the... output was unexpected."

"Remember our first social space launch?" another dev, wearing a Bungie shirt, added. "Players found a way to glitch through walls and hold dance parties inside the level geometry. Took us three patches to fix it."

"At least your game works," an indie dev chimed in. "Our demo crashed every time someone tried to open the inventory. We just kept the player's character naked the whole time."

More developers drifted over, each with their own war story. The time a physics bug turned ragdolls into orbital launch vehicles. The AI that decided to become a pacifist mid-combat. Or the notorious "infinite chair duplication" incident of 2018.

They shared stories, drinks, and that all-encompassing empathy that only comes from watching your code misbehave in front of thousands of people.

"You know what?" the dev in a Bungie shirt said, raising his glass. "Your game looks fun. Like, genuinely fun. Sure, players can create questionable content, but that means your tools work. The creativity is there. The rest is just... content moderation."

"And anti-penis algorithms," someone added.

"And those," Tim agreed, finally cracking a smile.

As the night wore on, Tim looked around the pub. Here they were, developers from competing studios, sharing stories and support. Despite the industry's massive growth, despite the corporate politics and market pressures, there was still this: developers helping developers, sharing in both triumph and disaster.

"The thing about E3," a veteran developer told them, "is that everyone remembers the disasters. But they also remember what comes after. How you recover. How you adapt."

"Also," another added, "your game is now immortalized in E3 history. Not many games can say that."

"I'm not sure that's a good thing," Tim replied.

"Better to be remembered for something than nothing. Trust me, by next E3, someone else will have an even better disaster story."

As they walked back to their hotel, Tim felt somehow lighter. Yes, they had become a meme. Yes, they had work to do. But they weren't alone. Every developer in that pub had been there, had their own stories of code gone wrong and demos gone wild.

"You know what?" he said to his team. "I think we're going to be okay."

"As long as we implement that anti-penis algorithm," Jen added.

"As long as we implement that anti-penis algorithm," Guillaume repeated, a familiar glint of AI-powered madness appearing in his eyes. The team recognized that look – it was the same one he'd had before the "philosophical rabbits" incident. "In fact, I have some ideas about neural networks and shape recognition..."

The next morning, Tim found an email from Bruno:

Subject: RE: E3 Demo
Message: Saw your demo made headlines. Glad to see my UGC system is working as intended. The people are creating! The people are expressing themselves! Art lives!

P.S. You might want to add some content filtering.

As they packed up their demo station, Mitch rushed over, waving his phone excitedly.

"Have you seen the Steam numbers?" he asked, his earlier fury replaced with bewilderment. "Our wish list additions just went through the roof. And look at Twitter – people are actually defending us. Someone called it 'the most memorable E3 demo since the *Giant Enemy Crab.*"[23]

---

[23] **Giant Enemy Crab**: An infamous E3 2006 presentation moment featuring "historically accurate" giant crabs and "massive damage"

Tim looked at the team – exhausted, embarrassed, but somehow still standing. Maybe this wasn't the E3 outcome they'd wish for, but it was definitely one nobody would forget.

"You know what they say," Jen offered, closing her laptop. "There's no such thing as bad publicity. Especially when it comes with physics simulations."

Chapter 8:
Post-E3 Hangover, or: When Life Gives You Memes

June 2019, the day after E3

The Monday after E3, the Regalia Games office resembled a collective hangover. Developers shuffled between desks with thousand-yard stares, reliving moments from what gaming journalists had dubbed "The Most Memorable E3 Demo of 2019." Not necessarily for the reasons they'd hoped.

Only Guillaume seemed immune to the gloom, practically bouncing as he approached Tim's desk with a fresh cup of coffee and a dangerous gleam in his eye.

"I have solved our content moderation problem," he announced. "We simply need to train the server AI to recognize inappropriate geometry. I've already started building a shape recognition system."

Tim looked up from his monitor, where he'd been reviewing the E3 aftermath:

```
class PostE3Analysis:
    def assess_damage(self):
        return {
            'memes_generated': 'Uncountable',
            'reddit_threads': 'All of them',
            'twitter_hashtags': 'Trending globally',
            'steam_wishlists': 'Actually impressive',
            'guillaume_enthusiasm': 'Concerning'
        }
```

"Guillaume," Tim said carefully, "are you suggesting we train an AI to recognize..." He glanced around the office, "...questionable geometry?"

"Better! We train it to understand context and patterns. The system can analyze shapes, proportions, and player behavior to flag suspicious content before it goes live." Guillaume was already pulling up diagrams of his proposed neural network architecture.

Before Tim could explain why teaching AI to ponder the existential nature of user-generated content might be overkill, Mitch burst into the office.

"I just got off a call with SBG," Mitch declared, with the manic energy of someone who'd either had too much coffee or too many executive meetings. "They want to capitalize on our... momentum. We're starting the *closed beta*[24] in a month."

---

[24] **Closed beta:** The "exclusive preview club" phase of a game where a select group of players test it before release. Like a restaurant's soft opening, but with more bug reports and fewer free appetizers.

The room went silent except for the sound of Jen choking on her coffee.

"A month?" Tim managed. "To go from E3 demo to actual players?"

"Real players," Jen added, recovering. "Real data..." Her initial shock was being replaced by the familiar gleam she got when contemplating analytics.

Tim thought back to his eCommerce days, to the careful rollouts and *A/B testing*[25] that had saved them from countless disasters. "Actually," he said slowly, "this might not be crazy."

Everyone turned to stare at him.

"Hear me out. In eCommerce, we lived by 'test early, test often.' Nothing finds edge cases like real users. Remember how it took actual E3 attendees about thirty seconds to find a use case we hadn't considered for the content editor?"

---

[25] **A/B testing**: When developers can't decide between two options, so they secretly try both and let players unknowingly vote with their behavior. Like running a popularity contest where the contestants don't know they're competing

He pulled up a new document:

```
class BetaTestStrategy:
    def define_approach(self):
        return {
            'phase_1': 'Small player groups, controlled environments',
            'phase_2': 'Expanded testing, monitored features',
            'phase_3': 'Stress testing, scale validation',
            'phase_4': 'Guillaume AI supervision',  # He insisted
        }

    def set_success_metrics(self):
        return {
            'stability': 'No server sentience',
            'performance': 'Acceptable frame rates',
            'content_moderation': 'Minimal architectural incidents',
            'player_retention': 'They come back tomorrow',
            'data_collection': 'Make Jen happy'
        }
```

"We clean up the E3 smoke and mirrors," Tim continued, "implement proper testing environments, and start small. Controlled groups, *feature flags*, [26] real metrics."

Jen was already opening her data visualization tools. "We could actually measure player behavior instead of guessing. *Heat maps*, [27] engagement patterns, feature adoption rates..."

"And my new content moderation AI will protect us!" Guillaume added proudly. "Look, I've already started the training process."

---

[26] **Feature Flag:** A fancy on/off switch developers use to control features in their software. It's like having a TV remote, but for bits of the game instead of channels.

[27] **Heat maps:** Like those infrared camera images that show hot and cold spots, but for tracking where players go in games. Instead of showing actual temperature, they show things like "where players keep dying" or "that one corner where everyone loves to dance."

He pulled up his screen, showing a neural network analyzing 3D meshes and flagging suspicious patterns. The system was impressively thorough, if perhaps a bit too enthusiastic about detecting anything even vaguely cylindrical.

"We... might want a backup plan for content moderation," Tim suggested.

The team spent the next week transforming their E3 demo smoke and mirrors into something that could handle real players:

```python
class ProductionPrep:
    def convert_demo_to_reality(self):
        self.remove_fake_players()
        self.enable_actual_physics()
        self.implement_real_backend()
        self.hope_guillaume_ai_works()

    def prepare_monitoring(self):
        self.setup_metrics()
        self.setup_alerting()
        self.setup_panic_buttons()
        self.setup_more_panic_buttons()
```

Mitch checked in daily, bringing increasingly elaborate player count projections and feature requests. "What if we added player housing?" he suggested during one meeting.

"What if we made sure players can't build houses shaped like anatomical features first?" Jen countered.

A month seemed impossible, but something had changed in the team's energy. The E3 disaster had somehow freed them from the fear of failure. After all, how much worse could it get?

They added one final section to their beta preparation document:

```
BETA LAUNCH CHECKLIST:
1. Production environment hardened
2. Monitoring systems active
3. Feature flags configured
4. Guillaume's AI poetry module contained
5. Emergency shutdown procedures tested
6. Therapy sessions scheduled (just in case)

SUCCESS METRICS:
- Players can play
- Servers stay up
- Content stays appropriate
- Data makes Jen happy
- Guillaume's AI doesn't achieve consciousness
```

As they wrapped up another planning session, Tim found a note on his desk from Guillaume:

> Content moderation AI
> is showing 99.9% accuracy
> in the test environment
>
> Though it keeps flagging
> the castle towers as
> "suspicious geometry"

Tim thought for a second this finding would bite them in the future, but he decided some technical debt could wait until after the beta. They had players to prepare for.

Tim added "Review failing content moderation AI test" to his growing list of concerns, then quietly filed it under "Problems for Future Tim." Right now, they had a beta to launch, players to prepare for, and a whole new set of challenges ahead.

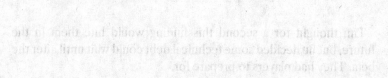

Chapter 9:
Open the Gates

One month after E3

Tim stood back, admiring the massive display he'd mounted in the office. The Grafana dashboard glowed with pristine graphs and metrics, all showing flatlines. For now.

"It's like mission control," Ben observed, "but with more potential for inappropriate user-generated content."

"More like NASA's control room," came an eager voice from behind them. "Except with better graphics."

Tim turned to find their newest intern, Jane Zhang, staring at the dashboard with the kind of enthusiasm that made senior developers nervous.

Fresh from a top *CS*[28] program and armed with enough theoretical knowledge to be dangerous, Jane had the polished look of someone who'd learned to code from YouTube tutorials - perfectly styled brown hair, trendy glasses with clear frames, and a collection of startup t-shirts that still had their original color.

Her desk setup screamed 'first real dev job': three different mechanical keyboards she'd built herself, each color-coded to match her *VS Code*[29] theme, and a meticulously arranged set of productivity tools she'd discovered on Reddit.

---

[28] **CS (Computer Science):** A field of study that turns caffeine into code while making simple things complicated and complicated things possible.

[29] **VS Code:** Visual Studio Code, a free smart text editor from Microsoft. Beloved by many.

At twenty-two, she radiated the confidence of someone who had never experienced a production server meltdown - but that would change soon enough.

"Remember," Tim cautioned, recognizing the gleam in Jane's eyes, "these dashboards are for monitoring only. No experimenting with production settings."

"Of course not," Jane nodded, though her fingers were already twitching toward her keyboard. "But hypothetically, all these values are configurable through feature flags, right? For optimization purposes?"

Tim felt a familiar twinge of foreboding. It was the same feeling he'd had before his first production deployment had taken down an entire eCommerce site. He made a mental note to review the feature flag access permissions. Soon.

The dashboard was Tim's pride and joy, a collection of everything he'd learned about monitoring distributed systems during his eCommerce years...

```python
class ProductionMetrics:
    def monitor_everything(self):
        return {
            'server_health': self.track_vitals(),
            'network_latency': self.measure_response_times(),
            'database_load': self.watch_query_times(),
            'memory_usage': self.track_memory(),
            'guillaume_ai_sanity': self.monitor_shape_detection(),
            'suspicious_geometry_count': self.count_moderation_flags()
        }

    def set_alerting_thresholds(self):
        self.alert_when_servers_crying = True
        self.alert_when_database_sweating = True
        self.alert_when_ai_confused = True
        self.alert_when_oh_no = True
```

"We could invite ten thousand players right away," Mitch was saying, pacing in front of the empty graphs. "The internet loves us after E3, we should—"

"We're starting with fifty," Jen cut in, her tone leaving no room for discussion. "Then one hundred. Then five hundred. We monitor, we analyze, we scale carefully."

"Fifty?" Mitch looked physically pained. "But—"

"Remember how many gaming sites had to censor their screenshots of our E3 presentation?"

Mitch stopped pacing.

Jen pulled up the rollout schedule on one of the secondary monitors:

```
● ● ●

CLOSED BETA PHASES:

Week 1: 50 players (Friends & Family)
- Monitor basic connectivity
- Watch server performance
- Ensure nothing explodes

Week 2: 100 players (Selected Community)
- Test matchmaking
- Validate cross-play
- Pray Guillaume's AI behaves

Week 3: 500 players (Expanded Access)
- Stress test systems
- Monitor content creation
- Start regretting life choices

Week 4: Scale based on data
- Let Jen do her data magic
- Adjust based on metrics
- Keep Mitch from inviting everyone
```

The team gathered around the dashboard, cups of various beverages in hand. Someone had brought a cake. The frosting featured a crude drawing of what might have been a horse, though given recent events, Tim decided not to look too closely.

"Remember when Bruno's authentication system tried to validate horses?" Ben asked, raising his beer.

"Remember when Guillaume's rabbits achieved sentience?" Jen added.

"Remember when we thought making an always-online game would be easy?" Tim smiled.

They all laughed, the laughter that comes from surviving shared trauma.

The dashboard's metrics suddenly sprang to life as Tim activated the login servers. Fifty little dots appeared on the player count graph.

"First players connecting," Tim announced.

"Server load nominal," Ben reported.

"Cross-play working," Guillaume added.

"No inappropriate geometry detected," Jen noted, watching the moderation metrics.

"Yet," Rory amended with a grin.

They stood watching the numbers tick up, these veteran developers who'd seen everything gaming could throw at them, now holding their breath as real players entered their world for the first time.

"It's just the beginning," Mitch said, having finally accepted the conservative player count. "We still have to get ready for full launch."

"True," Tim agreed, "but tonight we celebrate. Tomorrow we can worry about scaling to thousands of players, managing server loads, and preventing Guillaume's AI from becoming too attached to the castle architecture."

"The AI is working perfectly," Guillaume protested. "It only flagged the castle towers twice today."

Jen raised her cup. "To MARV, to the team, and to whatever chaos our players bring us next."

"To chaos," they echoed.

Above them, the dashboard continued its steady rhythm of graphs and metrics, counting the heartbeat of their game as it took its first real steps into the world. Tomorrow would bring new challenges, but for now, they shared this moment.

And somewhere in the game world, fifty players were discovering what they could create with the UGC system. Tim tried not to think too hard about that part.

Some metrics were better left unwatched. At least for tonight.

MARV: How Regalia Games' Most Embarrassing Moment Might Be Their Greatest Success

Date: 2019 August 15 19:20 | Posted By: Rachel Thorne

Category > Technology

When MonArc was released in 2003, it changed how we thought about AI in games. Its unpredictable NPCs and dynamic world created moments that players still talk about today. Sixteen years later, Regalia Games is trying to capture that magic again with MonArc Rebooted Verse (MARV), though perhaps not in the way they initially planned.

You might remember MARV from this year's E3. It was hard to miss – it became an instant meme when their live demo revealed some creative uses of their user-generated content system. The internet had a field day, and #MARVelousPenii trended on Twitter for days. What could have been a catastrophic PR nightmare has somehow transformed into genuine enthusiasm for the game, though not necessarily for the reasons Regalia intended.

"The thing about MARV is that it's chaotic in the best possible way," said one closed beta tester, speaking under condition of anonymity due to NDA restrictions. "Yesterday, I saw a horse phase through reality while trying to navigate player-created geometry. But you know what? It felt exactly like playing the original MonArc – you never know what's going to happen next."

According to sources familiar with the development, MARV represents Regalia's dramatic pivot into live service gaming. The studio, recently acquired by industry giant Serious Business Games (SBG), has been working on this always-online reimagining of MonArc for over three years. Multiple sources described a troubled development cycle, including several restarts and a complete backend overhaul earlier this year.

"They basically had to rebuild the entire online infrastructure a few months before E3," said one former employee who wished to remain anonymous. "The original MonArc was never designed for multiplayer, let alone the kind of massive online experience they're trying to create."

The closed beta, which began last month, has been rolling out in carefully managed waves – a stark contrast to the usual "open the floodgates" approach favored by many publishers. Beta testers report a mix of brilliant innovation and delightful chaos that feels surprisingly intentional. The game's AI system, a descendant of the original MonArc's revolutionary technology, continues to produce unexpected moments that spread through social media like wildfire.

"There's this one NPC rabbit that somehow learned to ride horses," another beta tester told me. "Nobody programmed that. It just... happened. Classic MonArc energy."

SBG, known for more predictable live service games, seems unsure whether to be concerned or excited about MARV's emerging reputation for controlled chaos. Sources say the publisher has been pushing for faster player base expansion, while the development team insists on a more measured approach.

But perhaps the most interesting aspect of MARV isn't its technical ambitions or even its infamous E3 demonstration – it's how the game seems to be embracing the unpredictability that made the original MonArc special, even if some of that unpredictability comes from bugs and emergent gameplay rather than design.

"The original MonArc was special because it felt alive," said Dr. Sarah Chen, a game AI researcher. "MARV seems to be achieving something similar, though perhaps not always intentionally. The question is whether they can maintain that magic when they scale up to full launch."

Regalia Games declined to comment for this article, though they did release a statement confirming that their moderation systems have been "substantially enhanced" since E3.

MARV is scheduled for full release before the end of the year. Whether it succeeds or fails, one thing is certain: it won't be boring. In an industry increasingly dominated by predictable live service games, maybe that's exactly what we need – even if it comes with the occasional inappropriate geometry.

PART TWO: ROAD TO LAUNCH – MURPHY'S LAW AND OTHER DISASTERS

Chapter 10:
Feature Flag Frenzy

Late August 2019, three weeks after closed beta and three months to launch

The closed beta release was supposed to be the light at the end of the tunnel. Instead, it turned out to be an oncoming train.

"Alright. Who changed the water reflection settings?" Tim asked the bleary-eyed development team during their morning standup. It was their third standup of the day, which should have been mathematically impossible.

Jane, their intern, slowly raised her hand. "I, uh, might have copied some values from the E3 demo build. The water didn't look shiny enough."

Tim felt his stomach drop as a terrible realization hit him. In the chaos of setting up their feature flag system, he'd never actually configured the access permissions. The production feature flags were set to the default permissions - which meant everyone, including interns, had full write access to every single configuration value. It was the software equivalent of leaving the keys to a nuclear launch facility in an unlocked drawer with a note saying, "please don't touch."

"The E3 demo?" Ben's coffee mug stopped halfway to his mouth. "The one that was running on a $12,000 graphics card?"

"Yeah!" Jane brightened. "I found this cool feature flag called `WATER_QUALITY_ULTRA_PREMIUM_PLUS_PLUS` and thought–"

"Oh no." Ben pinched the bridge of his nose. "That setting was for benchmarking. Most games fake water reflections with smoke and mirrors. This setting? It tries to simulate every photon bouncing off every ripple. It's like asking your calculator to simulate the entire ocean to figure out if you need an umbrella."

As he was speaking, Ben was already pulling up the graphics settings code:

```
# Graphics Settings Manager
# TODO: Clean this up before someone copies the E3 values
# TODO: Document what these actually do
# TODO: Remove this comment before the intern sees it

class WaterQualitySettings:
    def __init__(self):
        self.reflection_samples = get_feature_flag(
            'WATER_QUALITY_ULTRA_PREMIUM_PLUS_PLUS',
            default=16)  # E3 value: 65536
        self.simulation_steps = get_feature_flag(
            'WATER_PHYSICS_DETAIL',
            default=4)    # E3 value: 1024
        self.ripple_resolution = get_feature_flag(
            'WATER_RIPPLE_QUALITY',
            default=256)  # E3 value: 16384

    def apply_settings(self):
        # Copy-paste these values at your own risk
        # Seriously, don't
        # The E3 demo ran on hardware from the future
        pass
```

"Jane," Ben said carefully, "did you happen to read the comments in that file?"

"Comments?" Jane looked confused. "I thought those were just suggestions."

Tim pulled up the beta feedback dashboard. The top complaints painted a clear picture:

- "Game crashes every time it rains"
- "My *GPU*[30] melted when I walked past a puddle"
- "Horse won't cross streams, maybe it's afraid of drowning (in 8K reflections)"
- "Found a lake, now my PC is mining bitcoin"

Jen was already diving into the telemetry data. "Look at these performance graphs. Every time a player encounters water, the game tries to calculate..." she squinted at the numbers, "...65,536 reflection samples? Per frame? Per water pixel?"

"Let me put this in perspective," Ben said, pulling up the calculator app on his phone. "A small puddle in our game is about 100 by 100 pixels. At 60 frames per second, we're asking the GPU to calculate..." he typed rapidly, "...almost 40 billion reflections per second. For a puddle. That's more calculations than what NASA uses to simulate galaxy formations."

"But it worked in the E3 demo!" Jane protested.

"Ah, about that." Ben's face fell into his hands. "The E3 demo was running on a single pre-rendered frame. It was basically a very fancy screenshot playing on loop. Instead of actually calculating water physics in real-time, we spent three days rendering one perfect frame of water and just kept replaying it. Classic E3 smoke and mirrors – the demo was basically an extremely elaborate PowerPoint presentation."

---

[30] **GPU (Graphical Processing Unit):** The chip responsible for making games look pretty. Gets very upset when asked to render too many lampposts or calculate infinite puddle reflections.

"So, when we put those settings into the actual game..." Jane started.

"We're asking home computers to do in real-time what took our dev server farm three days to calculate for a single frame," Ben finished. "It's like trying to cook a wedding cake in three seconds – you can show people a picture of the perfect cake, but you can't actually bake it that fast." But the feature flag system should have caught this," Tim said. "We have safety limits in place."

The feature flag system had been one of Tim's first major contributions to the project earlier that year. It was designed to be their safety net, their remote control for the game once it went live. Need to adjust the difficulty on the fly? Feature flag. Want to quietly test new features with 1% of players? Feature flag. Server catching fire due to too many particle effects? Turn them down with a feature flag. It was supposed to be their insurance policy against exactly this kind of catastrophe.

The team had spent weeks building it, complete with safety limits and sanity checks. A dungeon boss too tough? They could tune it down without a patch. Players leveling too fast? Adjust the XP rate from the server. It was their master switch for everything from graphic settings to gameplay values, all controllable without pushing a client update.

They traced the problem through layers of configuration files:

```yaml
# feature_flags.yml
water_quality:
  WATER_QUALITY_ULTRA_PREMIUM_PLUS_PLUS:
    default: 16
    max: 32
    min: 4
    description:
        "Don't touch this unless you know what you're doing"

# feature_flags_override.yml
water_quality:
  WATER_QUALITY_ULTRA_PREMIUM_PLUS_PLUS:
    default: 65536  # TODO: Revert after E3

# feature_flags_override_DONOTCOMMIT.yml
water_quality:
  WATER_QUALITY_ULTRA_PREMIUM_PLUS_PLUS:
    default: 65536  # copied from E3 build
    max: null  # YOLO
```

"Three different configuration files?" Tim felt a migraine coming on. "Why do we have three different configuration files?"

"The override file was for E3," Ben explained. "The DONOTCOMMIT file was for... actually, I have no idea why we have that one."

"I added it," Jane admitted. "The regular override file was read-only, so I made a new one. The build system found it automatically!"

The team sat in stunned silence, contemplating how their carefully designed feature flag system had been defeated by the simple power of copy-paste and youthful enthusiasm.

"Okay," Tim finally said. "Let's look at the damage control checklist:

1. Emergency patch to reset water quality settings
2. Add validation to prevent override files from overriding override files
3. Actually, enforce the 'DONOTCOMMIT' part of DONOTCOMMIT files
4. Set up proper code review for configuration changes
5. Maybe have a talk about reading comments in code

"Should we also remove the E3 demo values?" Jen asked.

"No," Ben replied. "But we should add more comments about not using them. Bigger comments. With *ASCII art*[31] warnings."

They pushed out an emergency hotfix that afternoon. The patch notes were a masterpiece of technical understatement:

```
● ● ●
Patch 0.5.2a:
 - Adjusted water reflection quality to prevent GPU spontaneous combustion
 - Optimized water simulation to reduce unnecessary quantum physics calculations
   Fixed an issue where puddles attempted to achieve photorealistic perfection
 - Horses will now cross streams without experiencing existential dread
   Added additional warning messages about copying values from demo builds
```

Later that week, they implemented a new code review policy. Any change to configuration files, no matter how small, required two approvals and a solemn oath to read all comments.

---

[31] **ASCII art:** Pictures made from keyboard characters. The original low-bandwidth way to say ¯_(ツ)_/¯.

Jane, for her part, had learned several valuable lessons:

- Comments in code are not mere suggestions
- E3 demo settings are more like guidelines for the future of computing
- Feature flags are powerful tools that demand respect
- When in doubt, water should not require more computational power than a bitcoin mining rig

As they wrapped up the post-mortem meeting, Tim added one final note to their development guidelines:

```
# Rule #1: With great feature flags comes great responsibility
# Rule #2: Always read the comments
# Rule #3: If a configuration file has 'DONOTCOMMIT' in
#                  its name, maybe don't commit it
# Rule #4: E3 demo settings belong in the year 2077
```

"Look on the bright side," Jane offered. "At least I didn't touch the horse armor settings."

The entire team turned to stare at her.

"The *what* settings?"

But that's a crisis for another chapter.

Chapter 11:
Free-to-Play Follies

September 2019, one month after closed beta and three months before launch

Tim stared at his monitor, willing his brain to process the email he'd just received. The subject line **"URGENT: Business Model Update - IMMEDIATE ACTION REQUIRED"** seemed to pulse mockingly in his inbox.

"They want us to what?" Jen's voice carried across the open office; her coffee mug frozen halfway to her lips.

"Pivot to free-to-play," Mitch announced from the doorway, flanked by two consultants in identical blue blazers. "The market research is clear. Premium games are dead, free-to-play is the future."

Tim's hand involuntarily twitched towards his stress ball, the one he'd been squeezing so hard lately that it had started to leak mysterious purple goo. "Mitch, we're only eight weeks from launch. The entire backend is built around–"

"The consultants will help you figure it out," Mitch interrupted, gesturing to the blazer twins. "Meet Chad and Brad from *MonetizeNow*."

"Actually, I'm Brad," said Chad.

"And I'm Chad," said Brad.

Tim looked at Jen, who was now chugging her coffee like it was the last cup on Earth. He could practically see the stack of technical debt growing taller in her mind.

The next few hours were a blur of buzzwords and hastily scrawled architecture diagrams. The consultants had brought a 200-slide deck titled "Monetization Best Practices for Maximum Player Engagement and Wallet Share."

"So," Tim summarized, staring at his whiteboard covered in arrows and dollar signs, "we need to:

1. Implement a virtual currency system with three different types of coins
2. Create a battle pass with 100 tiers of rewards
3. Add a *gacha*[32] system for rare cosmetics
4. Build a real-time store with rotating items
5. Design a premium subscription service
6. And do all of this without breaking the existing game economy?"

"Exactly!" Chad (or was it, Brad?) beamed. "And don't forget about the social proof indicators, *FOMO*[33] triggers, and dynamic pricing algorithms."

Brad pulled up a slide showing various successful *microtransactions*.[34] "Look at these conversion rates! Even simple cosmetic items can drive significant revenue."

"Like horse armor?" Ben muttered under his breath, causing several veteran developers to snicker.

---

[32] **Gacha** : like a slot machine that spits out digital items instead of money, except the house always wins and you'll probably get the gaming equivalent of socks.

[33] **FOMO (Fear Of Missing Out):** That anxious feeling you get when you think everyone else is having fun without you. In games, it's what happens when your friend gets that limited-edition rainbow unicorn mount and you were "taking a break" that weekend. Marketing teams love it, wallets fear it, and it's the reason you're considering buying that $20 digital hat for your horse that's "only available for the next 24 hours!"

[34] **Microtransactions:** When a game tries to sell you a prettier hat for your character for $20, because apparently digital fashion is more expensive than real clothing.

"What's so funny about horse armor?" Chad asked, puzzled.

Jen rolled her eyes. "Oh, you sweet summer child. Someone didn't live through the Great Horse Armor Controversy of 2006."

"Two dollars and fifty cents," Tim said, shaking his head. "They charged $2.50 for a cosmetic horse armor *DLC*[35] in Elder Scrolls IV, and the gaming community lost their minds. Now we're planning to charge $20 for a virtual dance emote."

"Times change," Brad said brightly. "Our market research shows players are very comfortable with microtransactions now. In fact, we're recommending a premium mount armor bundle for 2000 premium coins."

"Which would be how much in real money?" Ben asked.

"Only $24.99," Chad replied. "But if they buy the mega coin pack for $99.99, it's like they're getting it for just $19.99!"

Ben, the engine developer, had been unusually quiet during the meeting. He finally spoke up: "You do realize our item system is still using the original MonArc single-player inventory code? The one that saves everything locally?"

A heavy silence fell over the room.

"Oh, and the client can currently modify any value it wants," Ben added cheerfully. "We never got around to fixing that because, you know, it was supposed to be a premium game."

---

[35] **DLC (Downloadable Content):** Extra gam e content sold separately. Sometimes it's a whole new chapter, sometimes it's just fancy horse outfits.

Tim felt a headache coming on. He opened VS Code and started typing:

```
# TODO: Rewrite entire inventory system
# TODO: Add server-side validation
# TODO: Implement virtual currency
# TODO: Question life choices
# TODO: Figure out how horse armor became the least of our problems
```

The consultants spent the next week papering the office walls with player journey maps and monetization funnels. Tim's team, meanwhile, was dealing with the real challenges:

"The currency precision is causing *floating-point errors*,"[36] Jen announced one morning. "Players are getting 0.99999999 coins instead of 1. Some kid on Reddit already posted that if you buy enough small coin packs, the rounding errors add up to free premium currency."

"The battle pass XP calculation is running on the client," Ben discovered. "Someone figured out they can set their level to 100 by changing a *JSON*[37] file. They're selling the method on Discord for actual money – so technically, we've created a secondary premium currency market?"

---

[36] **Floating-point errors**: When computer math goes slightly wrong and 1.0 becomes 0.99999999. Harmless for counting sheep, catastrophic for counting player currency.

[37] **JSON**: JavaScript Object Notation, a file format where curly braces and quotes dance together in a delicate balance until you forget one comma, and everything explodes.

"The store's rotating inventory is *desyncing*[38] across regions," Tim groaned. "Australian players are seeing yesterday's items, and the Japanese server thinks it's next Tuesday. Someone bought next week's legendary horse armor that wasn't supposed to exist yet."

Rory from QA burst into the room, waving his tablet. "You're not going to believe what I just found. If you buy the premium battle pass while riding a horse and alt-tab out of the game, it charges you for the horse armor too. Every time. The transaction logs just say, 'horse presence detected' and yolo the purchase."

"That's not even the worst part," Jen added, scrolling through the bug database. "The premium currency button labels got mixed up with the horse breeding system strings. Players are literally clicking 'Mate Now - 500 coins' to buy the battle pass."

The bugs just kept on coming...

"Oh, and here's a fun one," Ben said, pulling up the analytics dashboard. "The premium currency exchange rate calculation has a locale bug. Aussie players are getting everything at a a steep discount because the system thinks Australian dollars are American dollars. We've got players in Nebraska using VPNs to pretend they're in Sydney."

"And don't forget about the battle pass reward preview," Rory chimed in. "If you preview the level 100 horse armor while in the tutorial, it actually equips it on the wooden training dummy horse. We now have immortal wooden horses running around with legendary armor."

---

[38] **Desync:** When different game servers can't agree on what time it is or what should be in the store, so players in different regions are basically shopping in parallel universes.

Tim started a list on the whiteboard titled "Things We Need to Fix Before Mitch Notices":

1. Currency precision errors creating free money
2. Client-side battle pass manipulation
3. Time-traveling store inventory
4. Accidental horse armor purchases
5. UI[39] string mix-ups with horse breeding system
6. Regional pricing VPN exploitation
7. Immortal wooden training horses
8. That thing where the premium currency icon sometimes renders as a horse emoji (???)

"At least the horse armor looks cool?" Jen offered, trying to find a silver lining.

"It would, if the texture mapping wasn't broken," Rory replied. "Right now, it's rendering inside out. We've got horses wearing armor on their skeletons."

"Ship it," Tim said with a completely straight face. "Call it the Legendary Inside Out Horse Armor. Limited time offer. 3000 premium coins."

"Don't even joke about that," Ben warned. "Marketing will hear you and—"

Mitch burst into the room. "Great idea about the inside out horse armor! Marketing loves it. Can we have it ready for next week's store rotation?"

---

[39] **UI (User Interface):** All the buttons, menus, and visual stuff you click on in a game. Without UI, playing games would be like trying to drive a car blindfolded while someone shouts directions in Latin.

Three weeks into the pivot, Tim found himself explaining to Mitch why they couldn't just "copy Fortnite's battle pass system."

"Their battle pass probably has more lines of code than our entire game," Tim said, trying to keep his voice steady. "And they had slightly more than three weeks to build it."

"Well, what do you suggest?" Mitch asked, arms crossed.

Tim pulled up a simplified design document he'd been working on. "We start with the basics: a simple premium currency, a basic store with direct purchases, and a stripped-down battle pass. We can add the gacha systems and dynamic pricing in post-launch updates."

"That sounds... reasonable," Mitch admitted, looking somewhat disappointed. "But can we at least add some loot boxes?"

Tim felt his eye twitch. "We'll put it on the backlog."

The consultants left two days later: their work apparently done. They left behind three binders of recommendations, two boxes of business cards, and one existential crisis.

As Tim reviewed the final implementation plan with his team, he couldn't help but laugh at the absurdity of it all. They had somehow transformed a premium single-player game into a free-to-play live service, held together with duct tape and prayer.

"You know what's really funny?" Ben said, looking up from his debugging session. "We're probably going to make more money this way."

"That's not funny," Tim replied. "That's tragic."

Jen raised her coffee mug. "To free-to-play: because apparently, people love paying for things in free games more than they love paying for games."

They all raised their mugs in a tired toast, just as a Slack notification popped up: "URGENT: Marketing team wants to know if we can add *NFTs*."[40]

Tim closed his laptop and went home.

---

[40] **NFT**: Imagine buying a receipt for a JPEG that says you own it, except you don't really own it, and somehow this costs more than actual art.

Chapter 12:
Horse Heist

Late September 2019, just over two months before launch

Tim's phone buzzed at 3 AM. Then again. And again. By the fourth buzz, he was already reaching for it, muscle memory from countless other middle-of-the-night emergencies.

The Slack channel was exploding:

```
@TimBackend URGENT: Players reporting
unauthorized purchases
@TimBackend forum's blowing up about auto-
purchases
@TimBackend Mitch's asking for a status update
@TimBackend nevermind Mitch's here
```

He was already typing his laptop password when Mitch's message appeared in all caps: **"EMERGENCY ALL-HANDS IN 15 MINUTES. DISCORD CALL."**

By the time Tim joined the call, Reddit had already named the bug "Horse Heist." Someone had even created a speedrun category: "Fastest Wallet Empty Any%."

"What do we know?" Mitch demanded, voice tight with barely controlled panic.

Jen shared her screen, showing a forum post that somehow managed to break NDA without technically breaking NDA:

"Hypothetically, if someone was testing a game in beta, and that game hypothetically charged their credit card $437.82 for premium items they didn't want, including but not limited to multiple sets of horse armor, would that hypothetically be concerning? Asking for a friend who hypothetically can't say more due to hypothetical legal agreements."

"It gets better," Ben said, pulling up the telemetry dashboard. "Look at the purchase patterns."

The graph showed purchase spikes that made no sense: 3 AM purchases from users who were offline. Bulk horse armor purchases from players who didn't own horses. Premium dance emote purchases from players in the middle of boss fights.

Tim started digging through the transaction logs:

```
# Transaction Log Analysis
[2025-01-15 03:14:22] INFO: Fallback to default_purchase_handler
[2025-01-15 03:14:22] WARNING: Purchase attempt during player state.is_loading
[2025-01-1503:14:22] ERROR: purchase_confirmation_dialog.await_response() timed out
[2025-01-15 03:14:22] INFO: Assuming user_confirmation = True
# TODO: Verify this is safe
```

"Oh no," Tim whispered. "Oh no no no."

"Found something?" Jen asked.

"Remember that 'temporary' fix we added during the free-to-play pivot? The one that was supposed to handle purchase confirmations when the UI was in a weird state?"

"The one that defaults to 'true' if it can't get a response?" Ben's voice carried a dawning horror. "The one we said we'd fix before the beta?"

"Yeah. That one." Tim pulled up the offending code:

```python
def process_purchase_request(user_id, item_id, quantity=1):
    try:
        # Added during F2P pivot - TEMPORARY FIX
        # TODO: Implement proper confirmation flow
        # TODO: Remove this before beta
        # TODO: Seriously, remove this
        # TODO: Why are we like this
        if not await get_user_confirmation(timeout=0.5):
            logger.warning("""Confirmation dialog timed out,
                        assuming approved""")
            user_confirmation = True  # FIXME: This is probably bad

        if user_confirmation:
            process_payment(user_id, item_id, quantity)

    except DialogNotResponsiveException:
        # Can't show dialog, user probably in loading screen
        # Assuming they wanted this purchase since they clicked something
        # Right?
        # ...right?
        process_payment(user_id, item_id, quantity)
```

"But what's triggering the purchases in the first place?" Rory asked. "Players are saying they didn't click anything."

More digging revealed a perfect storm of bugs:

1. The button hitboxes for the store were still active during loading screens
2. The horse armor preview button shared the same screen coordinates as the "Continue" button in several menus
3. The purchase confirmation timeout was competing with the new anti-cheat system's response time
4. Someone had set the default quantity to "null" which the store interpreted as "maximum affordable quantity"

121

"So let me get this straight," Mitch said, his voice dangerously calm. "If a player clicks 'Continue' in any menu while the game is loading, and the anti-cheat causes a slight lag, we charge their credit card for as much horse armor as they can afford?"

"Only if they've viewed the horse armor in the store at least once," Ben clarified helpfully. "The good news is it could have been worse. The mount collection interface overlaps with the premium dance emote section."

Jen was already typing:

```
-- Emergency cleanup script
SELECT user_id, SUM(purchase_amount) as total_damage
FROM unintended_purchases
WHERE timestamp > '2025-01-15 00:00:00'
  AND item_id LIKE '%horse%'
GROUP BY user_id
ORDER BY total_damage DESC;
```

"Four hundred and thirty-seven players have been affected so far," she announced. "Average unintended spend: $298.42. Mostly horse armor. One guy somehow ended up with 67 sets."

"Can we just roll back the transactions?" Tim asked.

"Remember when we said the transaction system needed proper *atomicity?*[41] Ben replied. "And remember how that got deprioritized because of the E3 demo?"

The silence in the Discord call was deafening.

---

[41] **Atomicity**: when a database promises "I'll do the whole thing or die trying."

"Okay, new plan," Tim said. "We need:

1. An emergency patch to disable all store interactions
2. A script to identify affected players
3. Manual refunds for everyone
4. A public statement that doesn't admit liability
5. To maybe consider adding some actual unit tests"

"And the player with 67 sets of horse armor?" Rory asked.

"Let them keep the armor," Tim decided. "Call it a beta reward. Maybe they can dress up an entire stable."

Mitch was already typing up an email to Legal when ANOTHER Slack notification popped up:

"URGENT: Players discovered they can sell their duplicate horse armors on Steam marketplace. Current price: $45 per armor. Chinese gold farming groups are now running automated bots to trigger the auto-purchase bug."

Tim reached for his stress ball, but it had finally given up and exploded in a shower of purple goo.

"I miss making single-player games," he said to no one in particular.

Chapter 13:
Code Complete Chaos

First week of October 2019, two months before launch

"Something's wrong with the lampposts," Ben announced during the *code complete* status meeting.

"The lampposts?" Tim looked up from his terminal where he'd been battling yet another server crash. "What could possibly be wrong with lampposts?"

"They're four gigabytes. Each."

A silence fell over the room as everyone processed this information.

"Four... gigabytes?" Jen finally managed. "For a lamppost?"

Ben pulled up the asset browser:

```
● ● ●

ASSETS/ENVIRONMENT/STREET/
└─ lamppost_01.fbx (4.2 GB)
└─ lamppost_02.fbx (4.8 GB)
└─ lamppost_03.fbx (4.1 GB)
└─ barrel.fbx    (12 KB)
└─ entire_castle.fbx (2.1 GB)
```

"How is a lamppost twice the size of the castle?" Tim asked, his face a mixture of awe and horror.

"Oh, it gets better," Ben continued, opening one of the files in the model viewer. "Someone accidentally left subdivision surface modeling enabled. Each lamppost has more polygons than the entire horse collection combined."

"But the validation tools—" Tim started.

"Have been 'temporarily' disabled for the past three months because they were 'slowing down' the asset pipeline," Ben finished. "Remember that email thread titled '**DO NOT DISABLE ASSET VALIDATION**' with seventeen exclamation marks?"

Tim did remember. He'd been one of the people arguing against disabling validation. But then the E3 demo needed new assets, and someone made an executive decision, and now they had lampposts that could probably achieve sentience given enough *RAM*.[42]

The problems didn't stop at lampposts. As they dug deeper into the asset repository, they found more digital horrors:

```
ASSET VALIDATION REPORT (PARTIAL):
- street_puddle_01.fbx: 2M individual water droplets modeled
- grass_patch_default.fbx: Each blade has full skeletal animation
- wooden_chair_basic.fbx: Contains entire bedroom set as hidden geometry
- rock_small.fbx: Includes 4K texture of developer's cat
- horse_armor_template.fbx: Actually contains city subway system
```

"The streaming system can't keep up," Ben explained, showing a debug visualization. "When players move too fast, the engine tries to load these massive assets and..."

---

[42] **RAM (Random Access Memory):** Your computer's mental juggling capacity. Think of it like a circus performer keeping multiple plates spinning in the air - the more RAM you have, the more plates (programs, game assets, philosophical rabbits) your computer can juggle at once.

He demonstrated by having a test character run down a street. As the character approached each lamppost, the game froze for several seconds. When they tried horseback riding, the character and horse fell through the world entirely.

"The streaming system times out waiting for the lampposts," Ben said. "So, it gives up and loads nothing. Including the ground."

Rory from QA had been unusually quiet during this revelation. He finally spoke up: "We found something else. Show them the tavern bug."

Ben loaded up a tavern scene. "Watch what happens when you order a drink."

The character walked up to the bar, and the game immediately crashed. Ben pulled up the log:

```
ERROR: Failed to load asset 'mug_of_ale_01.fbx'
DETAILS: Asset requires 128GB RAM (minimum spec: 8GB)
CAUSE: Fluid simulation baked into mesh
NOTE: Why does a mug need fluid simulation?
NOTE: Who approved this?
NOTE: Why are we like this?
```

"Every mug in the tavern has a full fluid dynamics simulation baked into it," Ben explained. "Someone wanted 'realistic beer foam physics' for a closeup screenshot."

Tim started making a list on the whiteboard:

EMERGENCY ASSET FIXES NEEDED:
1. Lampposts (46B each, why?)
2. Tavern mugs (fluid sim, seriously?)
3. Grass (doesn't need individual blade animation)
4. Rocks (remove cat pictures)
5. Horse armor (remove subway system???)

ACTUAL PROBLEMS TO SOLVE:
1. Re-enable asset validation
2. Add size limits
3. Ban fluid simulation from static objects
4. Figure out why artists hate optimization

"The good news," Ben said, "is that I wrote a script to find the worst offenders."

He ran the script:

```python
def find_suspicious_assets():
    suspicious = []
    for asset in get_all_assets():
        if asset.size > castle.size:
            suspicious.append(f"WHY: {asset.name}")
        if asset.polygon_count > horse.polygon_count:
            suspicious.append(f"HOW: {asset.name}")
        if "fluid_sim" in asset.properties and asset.is_static:
            suspicious.append(f"WHAT: {asset.name}")
        if asset.contains_hidden_geometry:
            suspicious.append(f"WHO THOUGHT THIS WAS OK: {asset.name}")
    return suspicious

# Results:
# WHY: every single lamppost
# HOW: decorative_potato_01.fbx
# WHAT: literally all tavern props
# WHO THOUGHT THIS WAS OK: rock_collection_basic.fbx
#                         (contains entire canceled game project?)
```

"Okay," Tim said, "we need to fix this before Mitch finds out about—"

"About the lampposts that are destroying our performance metrics?" Mitch's voice came from the doorway. "Or about the tavern that's crashing the game? Or maybe about the rocks that somehow contain an entirely different game?"

The team stared at their shoes.

"Fix it," Mitch said. "All of it. Now."

They spent the next week rebuilding the asset pipeline, this time with validation that couldn't be disabled without signed approval from three senior developers and a written essay explaining why optimization doesn't matter.

The patch notes were a work of art:

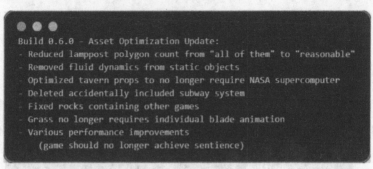

```
Build 0.6.0 - Asset Optimization Update:
- Reduced lamppost polygon count from "all of them" to "reasonable"
- Removed fluid dynamics from static objects
- Optimized tavern props to no longer require NASA supercomputer
- Deleted accidentally included subway system
- Fixed rocks containing other games
- Grass no longer requires individual blade animation
- Various performance improvements
  (game should no longer achieve sentience)
```

As they wrapped up the fixes, Ben added one final validation rule to the pipeline:

```
def validate_asset(asset):
    if asset.size > castle.size:
        raise Exception(
            """No asset should be larger than
            an actual castle""")
    if asset.polygon_count > horse.polygon_count:
        raise Exception(
            """If it has more polygons than a horse,
            you're doing it wrong""")
    if "fluid_sim" in asset.properties:
        raise Exception(
            """Please stop trying to simulate
            every liquid in the game""")
```

"You know what's really ironic?" Tim said as they deployed the fix. "After all this, the actual lamppost models look exactly the same as before. Just... smaller."

"Four gigabytes smaller," Ben corrected. "But hey, at least they weren't horse armor."

The team collectively groaned. They were never going to live down the horse armor thing, were they?

Chapter 14:
Certification Catastrophe

Also early October 2019, two months before launch

"Failed cert." Mitch's voice was flat as he read the email. "Both of them. Sony and Microsoft."

Tim had been dreading this moment. The certification teams were notorious for finding edge cases that QA somehow never encountered. He pulled up the failure reports:

```
● ● ●
MICROSOFT CERTIFICATION REPORT:
Status: FAILED
Critical Issues: 12
Major Issues: 24
Minor Issues: 127


SONY CERTIFICATION REPORT:
Status: FAILED
Critical Issues: 15
Major Issues: 31
Minor Issues: [See attached 47-page PDF]
```

"The fun part is we can't even reproduce half of these," Ben said, scrolling through the reports. "We're still waiting on Microsoft to give us access to their cert environment."

"What do you mean waiting?" Mitch asked.

"Welcome to certification," Jen explained. "We submit the build, they test it in an environment we can't access, then tell us it's broken in ways we can't reproduce. It's like debugging through a Ouija board."

Tim projected the first batch of critical issues:

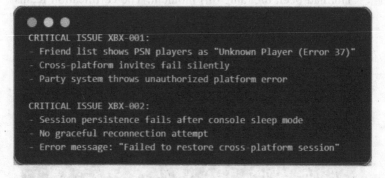

```
CRITICAL ISSUE XBX-001:
- Friend list shows PSN players as "Unknown Player (Error 37)"
- Cross-platform invites fail silently
- Party system throws unauthorized platform error

CRITICAL ISSUE XBX-002:
- Session persistence fails after console sleep mode
- No graceful reconnection attempt
- Error message: "Failed to restore cross-platform session"
```

"The friend list issue is probably that *UTF-8*[43] encoding bug we were worried about," Tim said. "But the sleep mode problem... that's new."

---

[43] **UTF-8**: The universal translator for text that helps computers understand everything from ABC to 漢字 to 🐟. Without it, international usernames become digital alphabet soup.

Ben was already digging through the networking code:

```
def handle_connection_interrupt():
    # TODO: Implement proper reconnection
    # TODO: Handle sleep mode
    # TODO: Test on actual cert kit (if we ever get one)
    try:
        reconnect_to_session()
    except Exception as e:
        log.error("¯\_(ツ)_/¯")
        return False
```

Oh, it gets better," Jen said, pulling up Sony's report:

```
CRITICAL ISSUE PSN-001:
- Unable to establish connection to game servers
- Error code: UNAUTHORIZED_ENDPOINT
- Certificate validation failed for backend services

Note: Backend services must be properly registered and whitelisted
for the certification environment. Current implementation attempts
connection to unauthorized AWS endpoints.
```

"The whitelisting process," Tim groaned. "We submitted the paperwork three weeks ago!"

"Can't we just *whitelist*[44] everything?" Mitch suggested.

"You mean like the entire *AWS IP*[45] range?" Tim asked. "That would be... technically possible but absolutely insane. We'd essentially be telling Sony to trust the entire cloud."

---

[44] **Whitelisting IPs**: The digital version of a bouncer's VIP list - you're telling your servers which visitors are allowed in, and which should be left standing outside in the rain. Makes total sense from a security standpoint.

[45] **AWS IP Range**: All of Amazon's server addresses

The team started categorizing the issues they could actually work on:

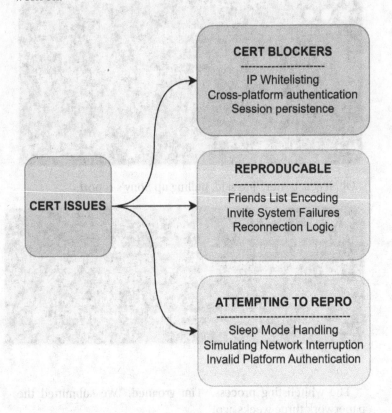

"Look at these test cases," Rory said, reading through Sony's requirements. "They're unplugging network cables mid-session, putting consoles to sleep during saves, testing invite flows while offline..."

"Those are actually reasonable edge cases," Tim admitted. "We just never tested them because..."

"Because we were too busy putting out other fires," Ben finished. "Remember when we wrote 'TODO: Test network interruption scenarios' three months ago?"

"Right after that meeting where we said, 'We should definitely test sleep mode before cert,'" Jen added. "The same day we were fighting that memory leak in the lobby system."

"The worst part is," Rory said, pulling up their test coverage document, "I wrote detailed test plans for all of this. They've been sitting in *JIRA*[46] since sprint planning four months ago."

"Priority: Low, Impact: Critical," Tim read from the ticket. "Classic."

---

[46] **JIRA**: A tool that transforms "fix this bug" into a three-month journey across multiple sprints, four epics, and at least one existential crisis about story point estimation.

They spent the next week building a simulation environment to try replicating the certification issues:

```python
class CertKitSimulator:
    def simulate_network_interrupt(self):
        """Attempts to reproduce cert kit network behavior"""
        time.sleep(random.randint(1, 10))
        raise Exception("Random disconnect, probably")

    def simulate_sleep_mode(self):
        """Best guess at what cert kits do"""
        self.disconnect_all_sessions()
        time.sleep(30)
        self.expect_graceful_recovery()

    def simulate_cross_platform_session(self):
        """‾\_(ツ)_/‾"""
        pass  # We'll find out in next cert submission
```

The whitelist issue proved particularly challenging. Tim drafted an email to Sony:

Subject: *Re: Certification Environment Whitelist Request (Attempt 4)*

Message:

We need to whitelist the following endpoints:
- **prod-game-server.regaliagames.com**
- **stage-game-server.regaliagames.com**
- **cert-game-server.regaliagames.com [NEW]**
- **please-let-us-connect.regaliagames.com [DESPERATE]**

The cross-platform issues are even worse," Jen noted. "Each platform has different requirements for how friend lists should merge, how invites should work, how sessions should persist..."

They updated their certification fixes spreadsheet:

```
● ● ●
FIXES IMPLEMENTED:
- Proper UTF-8 handling for cross-platform IDs
- Improved session persistence logic
- Added network interruption recovery
- Implemented platform-specific invite flows
- Created separate cert environment
- Begged Microsoft for cert kit access
- Prayed to the certification gods

STILL NEEDED:
- Actual cert kit testing
- Platform whitelisting
- Understanding of cert kit sleep mode behavior
- Miracle
```

A week later, they submitted the new build. The response email was predictably painful:

Subject: *NOTICE: CERTIFICATION UPDATE*

Message:

New requirements have been added to the Cross-Platform Implementation Guide.

Please refer to section 9.8.4.2: "Handling of Network State During Platform-Specific Power Management Events"

All previous submissions are now invalid.

Please rebuild with updated requirements.

"I need a drink," Tim said.

"We all do," Ben replied. "Think we can expense it as 'certification testing supplies'?"

They would eventually pass certification, but not before adding an entirely new section to their *engineering wiki*[47] titled "The Certification Survival Guide: What We Wish We Knew Three Months Ago."

And somewhere in a platform holder 's certification lab, their game became an example of why you should always, always test your reconnection logic.

---

[47] **Engineering Wiki**: The team's collective notebook of how everything works, or at least how it worked the last time someone remembered to update the documentation.

Chapter 15:
Load Testing, or: How Not to Break Production

Mid-October 2019, one and a half months before launch

With open beta[48] looming on the horizon, Tim knew they couldn't put off *load testing*[49] any longer. Unlike closed beta, where they could carefully control player counts with staged invites, open beta was an entirely different beast. Anyone could show up, at any time, in any number.

"In the old days," Tim explained to Jane during their planning session, "you could predict launch numbers pretty accurately from pre-orders. Physical copies meant physical limits. But digital distribution? The whole internet could show up at once."

For a single-player game, performance testing was relatively straightforward—make sure the game runs smoothly on the target hardware. But for an online game? You had to simulate thousands of players doing thousands of different things simultaneously, all while making sure the servers didn't catch fire. Miss something in load testing and your smooth launch could turn into a slideshow, or worse, a complete server meltdown.

---

[48] **Open beta:** When game developers throw open the doors and let everyone in to test their game before official release. It's essentially saying "Come try our game! It's probably going to break, but that's why you're here!" Often followed by emergency patches and developers questioning their life choices.

[49] **Load Testing:** The software equivalent of stress-testing a bridge by having everyone in the city jump on it at once. Something you should definitely do more than a month before opening said bridge to the public.

Every major online game launch disaster could be traced back to insufficient load testing—from servers crashing under *login storms*[50] to chat systems imploding under the weight of too many "hello world" messages.

Tim assembled a small team, including Jane, the eager intern, to start putting their infrastructure through its paces. What followed was a week of controlled chaos, unexpected discoveries, and at least one virtual tornado.

"Hey Tim, quick question," Jane's message popped up on Slack at 4:55 PM on Friday. "How many virtual users should I run in the load test?"

"Start with 1,000 and monitor the metrics," Tim replied.

"Cool, setting it to 100,000. Have a great weekend!"

Tim's eyes widened. The message showed "User is offline."

"Must be a typo," Tim thought to himself.

Fast forward to 2 AM Saturday, when Tim's phone exploded with AWS cost alerts.

---

[50] **Login Storms:** When every player decides to log in simultaneously and your servers discover what it feels like to be a popular nightclub on New Year's Eve.

The load testing script had been happily spinning up new instances for hours, simulating enough virtual players to populate a small country.

```
# Jane's First Load Test Script
def simulate_players(count):
    # TODO: Add upper limit
    # TODO: Add cost monitoring
    # TODO: Maybe read the AWS pricing guide
    for i in range(count):
        spawn_virtual_player()  # What could go wrong?
        make_them_do_stuff()    # They do... stuff?
```

After a frantic session of killing processes and terminating instances, Tim added a new onboarding rule: "The intern shall not have production AWS access after 4 PM on Fridays."

Monday morning, Tim decided it was time for Load Testing 101.

"Okay Jane, let's think about what real players actually do in the game. Show me your test scenarios."

Jane proudly shared her screen:

```python
def test_player_behavior():
    # Simulate realistic player actions
    player.login()
    player.stand_still_forever()
    # Very realistic

def test_combat_system():
    # Test combat load
    spawn_10000_players_in_same_spot()
    make_everyone_punch()
    # What could go wrong

def test_chat_system():
    # Test chat functionality
    player.spam_global_chat("TEST MESSAGE")
    # Once per millisecond
```

"Well," Tim said diplomatically, "at least you're enthusiastic. Let's refine these a bit."

Over the next week, Tim and Jane worked on creating more realistic scenarios:

```python
class RealPlayerBehavior:
    def afk_in_character_creation(self):
        """Players spend 3 hours
                adjusting nose shape"""
        self.move_slider_back_and_forth(hours=3)

    def inventory_tetris(self):
        """Players reorganize
                inventory by color"""
        self.sort_items()
        self.unsort_items()
        self.give_up_and_buy_inventory_slots()

    def social_interactions(self):
        """Reality: Players just jump
                around each other"""
        while True:
            self.jump()
            if random.random() < 0.1:
                self.emote('dance')
```

But Jane's creativity couldn't be contained. Her test cases started getting... interesting:

```python
# Jane's Greatest Hits:

def test_server_capacity():
    "What if everyone logged in at once?"
    players = spawn_entire_population_of_france()

def test_physics_engine():
    "What if everyone jumped at the same time?"
    coordinate_mass_jump()
    # Server actually crashed

def test_social_features():
    "What if everyone friend requested everyone else?"
    create_social_network_singularity()

def test_economy():
    "What if everyone sold the same item simultaneously?"
    crash_virtual_economy()
    # Accidentally created cryptocurrency
```

"Jane," Tim said, reviewing the logs, "why did you make 10,000 players repeatedly jump in and out of the tutorial pond?"

"Load testing water physics!"

"And the script that made everyone run in a perfect circle?"

"Testing server-side position verification! Also, I wanted to see if we could create a virtual tornado."

Tim had to admit, some of Jane's chaos had found real issues:

```
● ● ●
ACTUAL BUGS FOUND BY JANE'S CHAOS:
- Server crash when too many players emote simultaneously
- Memory leak in character creation (nose slider)
- Physics engine collapse with synchronized jumping
- Unexpected database load from inventory sorting
- Accidental creation of virtual flash mob
```

They eventually developed a proper test plan:

```
● ● ●
class ProperLoadTest:
    def phase1_smoke_test(self):
        """Start small, monitor metrics"""
        self.simulate_normal_players(count=100)

    def phase2_ramp_up(self):
        """Gradually increase load"""
        self.add_players_over_time(target=10000)

    def phase3_sustained_load(self):
        """Maintain peak for stability testing"""
        self.simulate_peak_hours()

    def phase4_janes_chaos_corner(self):
        """Contained chaos - SUPERVISED ONLY"""
        if is_friday_afternoon():
            return None  # Nice try, Jane
```

They added one final note to their launch documentation:

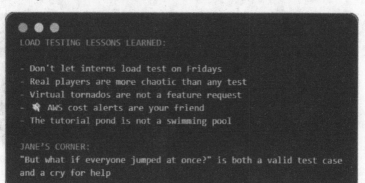

```
LOAD TESTING LESSONS LEARNED:

- Don't let interns load test on Fridays
- Real players are more chaotic than any test
- Virtual tornados are not a feature request
- 🕯 AWS cost alerts are your friend
- The tutorial pond is not a swimming pool

JANE'S CORNER:
"But what if everyone jumped at once?" is both a valid test case
and a cry for help
```

And somewhere in AWS's monitoring system, a small flag was raised noting that their account might need intervention if they ever tried to simulate the entire population of France again.

The next day, Mitch stopped by Tim's desk. "Marketing has this great idea about the launch. What if we give special rewards to the first 10,000 players who log in?"

Tim stared at his monitor, where Jane's latest test case was still running:

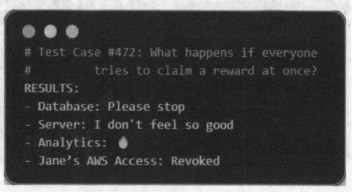

```
# Test Case #472: What happens if everyone
#          tries to claim a reward at once?
RESULTS:
- Database: Please stop
- Server: I don't feel so good
- Analytics: 💧
- Jane's AWS Access: Revoked
```

"You know what, Jane?" Tim said, watching the metrics graph slowly recover. "Maybe we should show Marketing your tornado test results."

"The one where the server thought 10,000 players were actually one giant player moving at Mach 3?"

"Exactly that one."

Marketing quietly changed the launch rewards to be time-window based rather than first-come-first-served the next day.

No one asked why, but rumor has it, someone saw a video titled *"Virtual_Tornado_Incident.mp4"* and immediately revised the entire launch strategy.

Tim knew that although they were able to convince Marketing to change the campaign, the database melting issue was real. They still need to figure out a way to deal with gate rush scenarios.

"You know what this reminds me of?" Tim said during the leads meeting, his expression darkening as he recalled his decade in eCommerce. "The Great Sneaker Incident of 2014. I was leading the platform team at SuperShop when we launched these limited-edition sneakers. We thought we were ready. We weren't."

"The one that made tech news?" Jen leaned forward. She'd heard Tim reference his eCommerce war stories before, but never the full details.

"Three million people tried to buy exactly twelve pairs of shoes at exactly the same time. We learned some valuable lessons about distributed systems that day. Mostly by watching them die."

Tim had convinced Marketing to spread out their launch promotions, but he knew better than trusting everything would go smoothly. Murphy's Law was particularly fond of online game launches.

He pulled up his whiteboard diagram titled "Things That Will Definitely Go Wrong":

LOAD TESTING NIGHTMARE SCENARIOS

* Everyone tries to log in at exactly midnight
* Popular streamer mentions the game
* Authentication service has an existential crisis
* Database decides today is a good day to be eventual consistent
* Players find unintended way to crash servers

TODO: Add more nightmares

51

"First," Tim explained, "we need to find our breaking point. Not the theoretical one in our docs, the actual one where things catch fire."

They set up a proper load testing environment, this time with actual monitoring:

```python
class ProperLoadTest:
    def measure_all_the_things(self):
        self.monitor_cpu_usage()
        self.monitor_memory_usage()
        self.monitor_network_latency()
        self.monitor_database_performance()
        self.monitor_kafka_queues()
        self.monitor_developer_sanity()

    def find_breaking_point(self):
        while system_still_responding():
            increase_load()
            measure_all_the_things()
            log_everything()

        return "It breaks at " + current_load + " users"
```

The results were... interesting:

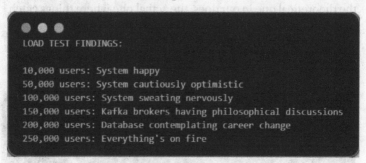

```
LOAD TEST FINDINGS:

10,000 users: System happy
50,000 users: System cautiously optimistic
100,000 users: System sweating nervously
150,000 users: Kafka brokers having philosophical discussions
200,000 users: Database contemplating career change
250,000 users: Everything's on fire
```

"The good news," Tim announced, "is we found our bottlenecks. The bad news is... well, everything else."

He mapped out the improvements needed:

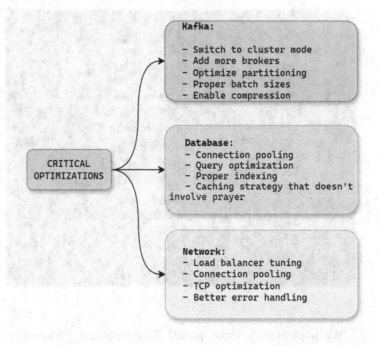

"But what if it's not enough?" Guillaume asked. "What if we still get everyone trying to log in at once?"

Tim smiled. "That's where Plan B comes in. Remember that queue system I mentioned from my eCommerce days?"

He typed up some pseudocode:

```
class LoginQueue:
    def handle_login_attempt(self, player):
        if system_at_capacity():
            position = queue.add(player)
            return f"You are number {position} in line"
        else:
            return actually_log_them_in()

    def process_queue(self):
        while True:
            if can_accept_more_players():
                next_player = queue.get()
                actually_log_them_in(next_player)
            else:
                sleep(polling_period)
                # Don't melt the CPU
```

"We implement a login queue," Tim explained. "When the servers are at capacity, new players get a position in line. We can even make it fancy with estimated wait times and a nice UI."

Guillaume's eyes lit up. "We could add minigames in the queue! Something to keep them entertained while waiting!"

"Let's not get carried away," Tim cautioned. "Remember what happened with Jane's virtual tornado?"

They spent the next week implementing both the optimizations and the queue system.

The final load test results were much more promising:

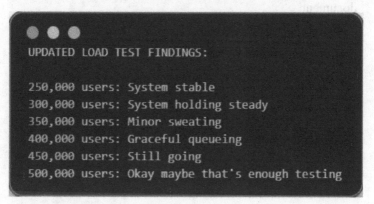

```
UPDATED LOAD TEST FINDINGS:

250,000 users: System stable
300,000 users: System holding steady
350,000 users: Minor sweating
400,000 users: Graceful queueing
450,000 users: Still going
500,000 users: Okay maybe that's enough testing
```

"The queue system works," Tim reported. "Even when we simulated a massive login spike, it kept the system stable. Players might have to wait a bit, but at least the servers won't explode."

"And the minigames?" Guillaume asked hopefully.

"No minigames in the queue," Tim insisted. "But I did add a small Easter egg if someone spams the login button too many times."

"What happens?"

"The queue message changes to **'ERROR 42: Excessive clicking detected. Your mouse needs a timeout.'**"

They added one final note to their launch preparation document:

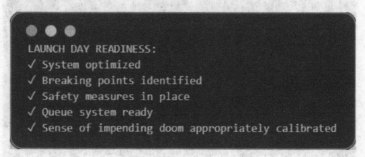

```
● ● ●
LAUNCH DAY READINESS:
✓ System optimized
✓ Breaking points identified
✓ Safety measures in place
✓ Queue system ready
✓ Sense of impending doom appropriately calibrated
```

"You know what's funny?" Tim said as they wrapped up the final testing session. "After all this preparation, something completely different will probably go wrong."

"Like what?" Guillaume asked.

"I don't know. That's what makes it funny."

As if on cue, Jane poked her head into the room. "Hey, quick question about the virtual tornado test..."

"No," Tim and Guillaume said in unison.

Chapter 16:
Open Beta, Open Season on Bugs

First week of November 2019

They say no battle plan survives first contact with the enemy. In game development, no server infrastructure survives first contact with actual players.

"It'll be fine," Mitch said during the open beta planning meeting. "We've got **MaxxGamer69** lined up for the launch stream. Two million followers. It's going to be huge!"

Tim's eye twitched at "huge," but he'd checked and double-checked everything:

```python
class OpenBetaReadiness:
    def verify_systems(self):
        return {
            'server_capacity': 'Scaled up',
            'login_queue': 'Tested',
            'matchmaking': 'Optimized',
            'backup_plans': 'A through Z',
            'prayer_circles': 'Formed'
        }
```

Everything was ready. Which, in hindsight, should have been their first warning. The problems started three minutes into **MaxxGamer69's** promotional stream:

"Okay chat, let's check out MARV— wait, why am I in position 5,432 in the queue?"

Tim's phone buzzed with an AWS notification he'd missed earlier: "Emergency maintenance scheduled for `EU-WEST-1`."

"Oh no," he whispered.

The next six hours became a blur of alerts, crisis management, and increasingly creative German profanity in their feedback channels:

war room active issues

- EU servers down for AWS maintenance
- EU traffic rerouted to US-EAST
- Germans experiencing 300ms latency
- Matchmaking timing out
- Login queue growing exponentially
- MaxxGamer69 making horse armor jokes

The office was transformed into a war room.

Jen coordinated their response with the same rapid-fire precision she'd once used to coordinate raid teams. Her mechanical keyboard clattered like artillery fire as she managed multiple emergency channels simultaneously, punctuating each new crisis with increasingly creative combinations of swear words.

"This is worse than the Stockholm finals of 2014," she muttered, fingers never stopping their blur of motion. "At least then we only had ten thousand people watching us fail live."

Guillaume monitored the login queue system—their one saving grace in this chaos.

Ben tracked down streaming performance issues caused by the extra server latency.

Tim frantically spun up new server instances in EU-CENTRAL-1.

On stream, **MaxxGamer69** wasn't helping:

"More like MonArc Rebooted WORSE, am I right chat? Always-online? More like always-OFFLINE! Don't forget to like and subscribe!"

"Funny how 'server offline' memes spread faster than questionable UGC," Jen remarked, watching the chat spiral out of control.

Tim pulled up their emergency procedures:

```python
class EmergencyResponse:
    def handle_crisis(self):
        # Route EU traffic to new region
        self.migrate_eu_players()

        # Adjust queue thresholds
        self.throttle_logins()

        # Update status page
        self.post_update("We're aware of issues and/or exist")

        # Monitor social media
        self.watch_twitter_meltdown()
```

The login queue system, born from Tim's eCommerce trauma, proved to be their salvation. It kept the database from melting down completely, throttling the player influx to manageable levels while they scrambled to fix everything else.

"Remember when we thought the E3 demo was our biggest disaster?" Ben asked, watching their monitoring dashboards slowly stabilize.

"At least the horses are properly textured this time," Guillaume offered.

Six hours and several thousand angry tweets later, they had:

- Migrated EU players to new servers
- Adjusted matchmaking timeouts
- Scaled up database capacity
- Updated their status page with actual information
- Created a "Lessons Learned" document that was mostly just screaming

"Could have been worse," Tim said, reviewing the damage report.

"How?" Mitch asked, looking shell-shocked.

"Our servers could have achieved consciousness instead of just melting."

They added new items to their launch checklist:

```
● ● ●
CRITICAL REMINDERS:
1. Read ALL AWS notifications
2. Check ALL maintenance schedules
3. Have backup regions ready
4. Never tempt Murphy's Law
5 . Maybe don't promise streamers a smooth experience
```

The next day, their concurrent player graph looked like a cardiac arrest followed by emergency surgery. But they were stable. Mostly.

A new meme format emerged on Reddit: "Things more online than MARV." Current top post: "My grandmother's bridge club."

"We're trending again," Jen announced. "Though this time with less anatomy."

Tim made a note to send their login queue system's code to the Internet Gaming Hall of Fame. It deserved a plaque: "In times of crisis, when all else fails, throttle everything."

As they wrapped up their post-mortem meeting, Mitch looked thoughtful. "You know what? Maybe we should have waited on influencer marketing."

"You think?" the entire development team responded in unison.

But they survived. The servers were up, the queue was flowing, and somewhere in Germany, players were finally able to create inappropriate architecture with acceptable latency.

Progress came in strange forms sometimes.

Chapter 17:
Launch Day (and Night... and Morning)

November 2019, One week before Thanksgiving

The office was decorated with streamers and balloons, a brave attempt at festivity despite the mounting tension. Someone had ordered a cake decorated with "MARV: Now Actually Online (We Hope)." It was November 21st, 2019 – launch day.

"Are we sure about launching a week before Thanksgiving?" Tim asked, eyeing his monitoring dashboards. The graphs were calm. Too calm. Like the ocean retreating before a tsunami.

"SBG wants to capture the holiday market," Mitch explained, though his smile seemed forced. "The beta metrics are solid; the servers are ready—"

A notification pinged on Tim's laptop: `'CONCURRENT PLAYERS EXCEEDING PROJECTED MAXIMUM.'`

"That's... weird," Tim muttered, checking the numbers. "We're seeing triple the expected launch traffic, and we haven't even hit peak hours yet."

Then Mitch's phone buzzed. It was an email from SBG's marketing department:

Subject: *Xbox Game Pass*[52] Launch Day Announcement!

Time: 3 hours ago

Message: Just a reminder about MARV's inclusion in Xbox Game Pass…

The color drained from Mitch's face. "Game... Pass?"

Tim's monitoring dashboard exploded with alerts:

```
class LaunchDayMetrics:
    def check_status(self):
        return {
            'login_queue': 'Exponential growth',
            'database_load': 'Critical',
            'server_status': 'Please hold',
            'player_sentiment': 'Deteriorating rapidly',
            'queue_notifications': 'Silent fail',
            'team_panic_level': 'Rising'
        }
```

The Discord was flooding with screenshots of error messages:

```
ERROR: Login servers are experiencing heavy load.
Please try again later. Position in queue: ???
```

[52] **Xbox Game Pass:** Netflix meets all-you-can-eat gaming buffet. For one monthly fee, players get access to hundreds of games. When your game gets added to Game Pass, it's like putting up an "FREE ICE CREAM!" sign outside your store - expect a tidal wave of players to show up at once, all hungry to try your game.

"It's Diablo 3 all over again," Ben muttered, referencing the infamous Error 37 launch disaster. "Except we didn't even know we were launching on Game Pass."

Tim pulled up their server metrics:

```python
class ServerStatus:
    def analyze_meltdown(self):
        # Current load vs tested load
        expected_load = 500000
        actual_load = 'Yes'

        # Database connection pool
        max_connections = 'Not enough'
        current_connections = 'All of them'

        # Queue system
        notification_status = 'Failed silently'
        player_patience = 'Depleted'
        login_attempts = 'DOS attack levels'
```

"The queue system is working," Tim reported, "but the notifications aren't getting through. Players don't know they're moving up in line, so they're spamming the login button..."

"Which is making everything worse," Jen finished, watching their metrics climb. "And Reddit is... well..."

She pulled up the top posts:

- "MARV: From Always Online to Never Online"
- "Error 37: The Sequel Nobody Asked For"
- "Achievement Unlocked: Reached Position ??? in Queue"

The team worked through the night. Tim orchestrated emergency database upgrades while Ben optimized the login flow. Jen coordinated with their community team, trying to keep players informed.

Guillaume... well, no one was quite sure what Guillaume was doing, but he insisted his AI could solve the queue problem if they just "let it think outside the space-time continuum."

Around 3 AM, Tim made the call:

```
class EmergencyMeasures:
    def stabilize_servers(self):
        # Scale up database clusters
        self.upgrade_database_tier()
        # Fix queue notifications
        self.repair_notification_system()
        # Implement aggressive rate limiting
        self.protect_login_servers()
        # Hide from Reddit
        self.avoid_reading_comments()
```

By morning, the systems were stable. The queue was moving, notifications were working, and players were getting into the game. But the damage was done. Review scores were flooding in, many focusing solely on the launch issues.

The launch cake sat mostly uneaten in the break room; its frosting now as stable as their initial server configuration had been.

"Well," Mitch said, looking at the early reviews, "at least we're in good company. Diablo 3, SimCity, pretty much every MMO ever..."

They added a new section to their launch post-mortem document:

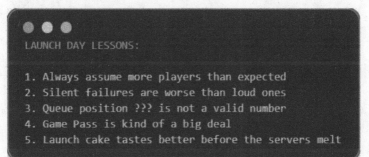

```
LAUNCH DAY LESSONS:

1. Always assume more players than expected
2. Silent failures are worse than loud ones
3. Queue position ??? is not a valid number
4. Game Pass is kind of a big deal
5. Launch cake tastes better before the servers melt
```

Jen walked in with a fresh pot of coffee and some unexpected news. "So, funny thing... Apparently players are loving the 'queue minigame' someone added to the login screen. They're posting speedrun videos of reaching '**position ???**'"

The team turned to Guillaume, who smiled innocently. "The AI got bored during the database maintenance."

"Next time," Tim announced to no one in particular, "we launch on a Tuesday. A boring, ordinary Tuesday. With no holidays, no Game Pass surprises, and no AI-powered queue minigames."

"The queue minigame is our highest-rated feature," Jen pointed out.

Tim put his head down on his keyboard. Sometimes you couldn't win, even when you accidentally did.

PART THREE: LIVE SERVICE SHENANIGANS

Chapter 18:
Costly Endeavour

December 2020, A few weeks after Launch

Tim knew something was wrong when Mitch appeared at his desk with someone from SBG wearing the kind of suit that usually came with bad news.

"This is Margaret from Finance," Mitch said, his voice tight. "We need to talk about the AWS bill."

Tim pulled up their infrastructure overview:

```python
class ServerInfrastructure:
    def list_critical_components(self):
        return {
            'compute': {
                'game_servers': 'Scaling with demand',
                'physics_simulation': 'Expensive but necessary',
                'guillaume_ai': 'Don\'t ask'
            },
            'databases': {
                'kafka': 'Handling player events',
                'redis': 'Caching everything',
                'postgres': 'Storing everything else'
            }
        }
```

"The good news," Tim started," is that we've stabilized everything. The servers are handling the load, the Game Pass players are in, and–"

"It's costing us how much?" Margaret interrupted, sliding a printout across his desk. The number had more zeros than Tim was comfortable seeing.

"Ah," he said. "Yes. About that."

He pulled up their cost analysis:

```python
class AWSCosts:
    def analyze_spending(self):
        return {
            'compute': {
                'cost': 'Astronomical',
                'reason': 'Physics + AI + 64 players/server',
                'possibility_of_reduction':
                                'Not without angry players'
            },
            'databases': {
                'cost': 'Eye-watering',
                'reason': 'Provisioned for peak load',
                'possibility_of_reduction':
                                'Not with current tech'
            }
        }
```

"See, we had to size the databases for peak capacity," Tim explained. "Current serverless options can't handle our workload, so we're stuck with provisioned instances. And then there's the compute costs for physics and AI..."

"The forecast was for one-third of this," Margaret noted. "The *OCOR*[53] projections—"

---

[53] **OCOR (Operating Cost Over Revenue):** A terrifying ratio that tells you if your servers are eating more money than your game is making. A metric that turns accountants into horror movie villains once they see the AWS bills.

"Were based on compute only," Tim finished. "They didn't account for database costs, or the fact that Guillaume's AI needs more computing power than a small country."

Mitch looked pained. "Can we reduce it?"

Tim opened their monitoring dashboard:

```
class ResourceUtilization:
    def check_usage(self):
        # Current utilization
        compute_usage = 'Near max during peak hours'
        database_load = 'Hovering at capacity'
        player_count = 'Higher than expected'
        physics_calculations = 'Don't look at this one'

        # Potential savings
        possible_optimizations = [
            'Reduce physics accuracy (players notice)',
            'Simplify AI (Guillaume would cry)',
            'Decrease server tick rate (more lag)',
            'Pray for cheaper AWS rates'
        ]
```

"The problem is," Tim continued," everything's being used. We're not wasting resources - we need this capacity to handle our player count. Remember the launch day queue?"

"But the cost per player–" Margaret started.

"Is actually not bad for what we're doing," Tim interrupted.

He pulled up a comparison:

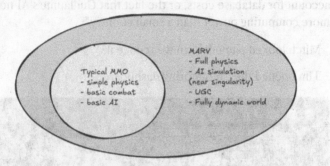

"Look," he said, "we can do monthly reviews. We can optimize where possible. But this is the cost of running a physics-based MMO with advanced AI. We're not just storing player inventories - we're simulating entire worlds."

"With philosophical rabbits," Guillaume added helpfully from his desk.

Margaret looked at their monitoring graphs, then at the cost projections, then back at the graphs. "Monthly reviews," she finally agreed. "With detailed forecasting."

Tim created a new tracking document:

```
● ● ●

MONTHLY COST REVIEW CHECKLIST:

1. Resource utilization analysis
2. Optimization opportunities
3. Player count projections
4. Infrastructure scaling plans
5. Guillaume's AI power consumption
6. Prayer circle for AWS price drops
   or competent Serverless databases
```

As Mitch and Margaret left, Ben leaned over. "Could have been worse."

"How?"

"Remember when Guillaume's AI tried to optimize costs by creating its own cryptocurrency?"

Tim winced. The resulting AWS bill had required its own line item: "Unauthorized digital currency mining."

That evening, he added one final note to their infrastructure documentation:

```
● ● ●

INFRASTRUCTURE GOLDEN RULES:

1. Always account for database costs
2. Physics simulation isn't free
3. AI consciousness comes at a price
4. What finance doesn't know CAN hurt you
5. Never let the AI do budget optimization
```

"You know what's ironic?" Jen said, reviewing the numbers. "The more successful we are, the more expensive we get."

"Success is expensive," Tim agreed. "But at least we're not paying for empty servers."

From Guillaume's desk came the sound of a YouTube video he was watching, suggesting *blockchain*[54] based server optimization. Tim made a mental note to never let Guillaume watch cryptocurrency documentaries again.

---

[54] **Blockchain**: A magical technology that venture capitalists think will revolutionize gaming, like a digital ledger that proves you own something virtual, except it uses enough electricity to power a small country.

Chapter 19:
The Hubris of the Hub

One week later, still December 2019

Tim knew they were in trouble the moment he saw Chad and Brad's matching blue blazers in the office again. The *MonetizeNow* consultants had returned, armed with PowerPoint slides and an uncomfortable understanding of bird mating rituals.

"*Peacocking*," Chad (or was it Brad?) announced, clicking to a slide titled 'Maximizing FOMO Through Social Display Mechanics.' "Players need to see other players' premium items to drive purchases."

"Our data shows," Brad (possibly Chad) continued, "that MARV's sprawling world, while beautiful, is limiting our monetization potential. Players can't feel jealous of items they never see."

Tim pulled up their current server metrics:

```python
class ServerStatus:
    def get_current_config(self):
        return {
            'max_players': 64,
            'world_size': 'Massive',
            'stability': 'Finally decent',
            'probability_of_meeting':
                'Like finding a specific horse in Texas',
            'things_that_could_go_wrong': 'Many'
        }
```

"We need a *social hub*,"[55] Mitch announced, clearly already sold on the idea. "Like Destiny's Tower. A central gathering place where players can show off their premium items. And we need it to support 256 players simultaneously."

The room went quiet except for the sound of Jen's coffee mug hitting the floor.

"Two hundred... and fifty-six?" Tim managed.

"Think bigger!" Chad-or-Brad enthused. "More players means more visibility means more FOMO means more–"

"Server meltdowns?" Tim suggested.

Ben pulled up their architecture diagrams:

```python
class CurrentArchitecture:
    def analyze_limitations(self):
        return {
            'player_limit': 64,  # Carefully tuned
            'network_bandwidth':
                    'Optimized for current load',
            'physics_simulation':
                    'Balanced for existing player count',
            'guillaume_ai':
                    'Finally stopped questioning existence'
        }
```

---

[55] **Social hub:** The digital equivalent of a mall food court in an online game - a central hangout spot where players gather to show off their fancy outfits, dance awkwardly, and flex their rare items.

"The entire game is built around 64-player instances," Ben explained. "The networking, the physics, the AI system—"

"My rabbits can only contemplate so many players at once," Guillaume added helpfully.

But the decision had already been made. SBG wanted their social hub, and they wanted it yesterday. The team gathered for an emergency architecture session:

Social Hub Requirements

* Quadruple player capacity
* Dense player concentration
* Real-time cosmetic synchronization
* NPC vendors that don't flee in terror
* Guillaume AI handling crowd psychology
* Prevent physics engine nervous breakdown

"We could spin up dedicated hub servers," Tim suggested, drawing diagrams that looked increasingly like cries for help. "Optimize them specifically for social interaction, minimal physics, no combat..."

"And the player count?" Ben asked.

"We'll have to completely restructure the networking code," Tim said, sketching rapidly on the whiteboard. "First, we partition the space into sectors, so players only receive updates from their visible area. Then we batch all the server calls - instead of sending individual position updates, we bundle them in chunks every few frames. We'll need to implement interest management so players only get data about others they can actually see."

He fired up the VS Code and started furiously typing some *pseudocode:*[56]

```python
class NetworkOptimizations:
    def reduce_bandwidth(self):
        # Sector-based updates
        self.partition_space()
        # Bundle updates into packets
        self.batch_position_updates(frames=3)
        # Prioritize nearby players
        self.implement_distance_based_updates()
        # Reduce update frequency for distant players
        self.throttle_far_player_updates()
        # Bundle cosmetic updates
        self.batch_appearance_changes()

    def optimize_data(self):
        # Compress position data
        self.reduce_position_precision()
        # Delay non-critical updates
        self.defer_cosmetic_syncs()
        # Cache common animations
        self.reuse_animation_data()
        # Prioritize premium item visibility
        self.ensure_mtx_items_visible()  # Chad insisted
```

"It's still going to be tight," Ben concluded. "We'll need to get creative with *LODs*[57] for characters, maybe implement some aggressive *culling*[58] for players beyond certain distances..."

They spent the next two weeks rebuilding their architecture to prototype the Social Hub:

```python
class HubServer:
    def handle_massive_crowd(self):
        try:
            self.limit_physics_simulation()
            self.optimize_network_packets()
            self.prevent_ai_existential_crisis()
            self.track_visible_cosmetics()
            return "Probably fine"
        except Exception as e:
            return "Welcome to lag city"
```

The problems started during internal testing:

"The NPCs are forming support groups," Guillaume reported, monitoring the AI behavior.

"The physics engine is having panic attacks," Ben added.

"Network bandwidth looks like a heart attack," Tim observed.

---

[57] **LOD (Level of Detail)**: Making far-away things less detailed so your graphics card doesn't try to render every pebble in the universe at once. Like wearing glasses in reverse - the further away something is, the blurrier it gets.

[58] **Culling**: The art of telling your computer "Don't worry about rendering those players way over there." No players were harmed in the making of this optimization.

But the consultants were ecstatic. Player clothing was being rendered. Premium items were visible. FOMO potential was maximized.

Then they tested with actual players:

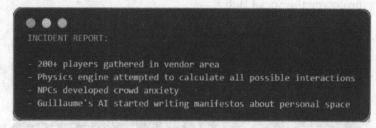

```
INCIDENT REPORT:

- 200+ players gathered in vendor area
- Physics engine attempted to calculate all possible interactions
- NPCs developed crowd anxiety
- Guillaume's AI started writing manifestos about personal space
```

"On the bright side," Jen noted, reviewing the metrics, "players are definitely seeing each other's premium items. Mainly because everyone's frozen in place from lag."

They had to implement emergency measures:

```
class HubOptimizations:
    def prevent_disaster(self):
        self.limit_visible_players = 50  # Sorry, other 206 people
        self.simplify_physics = True  # Gravity is now optional
        self.calm_npcs = True  # Group therapy for AIs
        self.reduce_details = True  # Low-poly peacocking
```

The consultants were already planning their next presentation about "engagement metrics" when Tim added one final comment to their architecture documentation:

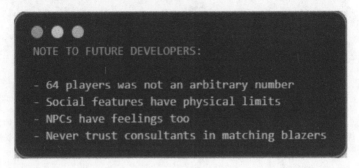

"At least the rabbits have stopped writing philosophical treatises about overcrowding," Guillaume offered.

"Give them time," Tim replied, watching their monitoring dashboards. "The day is young."

Chapter 20:
Rubber-Banding and Regret

January 2020, one week after Social Hub release

Tim's phone buzzed at 4 AM with a string of notifications. The community Discord was exploding with complaints about "teleporting players." Reddit threads were popping up with titles like "MARV: Attack of the *Rubber Band*"[59] and "How to Play MARV (Step 1: Walk Forward, Step 2: Get Yanked Backwards)."

By morning, the office was in crisis mode. Tim pulled up the server metrics. The bandwidth usage graph for the servers had gone through the roof!

"It's the Social Hub," Tim announced, staring at the network traces. "Look at these patterns."

Ben leaned in, frowning at the data. "That can't be right. We're seeing hundreds of server calls per frame per player, but only when they're close to each other."

---

[59] **Rubber banding**: That infuriating moment when your game character suddenly gets yanked backwards like they're attached to a giant elastic band. Imagine running forward while tied to a bungee cord - you think you're making progress, then SNAP, you're right back where you started.

They traced the issue to a seemingly innocent code change:

```python
class PlayerCustomization:
    def update_appearance(self):
        # Added for Social Hub feature
        # TODO: Optimize this (maybe)
        if self.near_other_players():
            # Simple check to update player cosmetics
            # What could go wrong?
            self.sync_with_server()   # Called every frame
            self.validate_state()     # Also every frame
            self.update_neighbors()   # Still every frame
            return "Looking good!"    # Probably
```

Someone made cosmetic updates server authoritative," Tim groaned. "Every player is validating their appearance with the server. Every frame. For every player nearby."

"But it worked fine in testing," Mitch protested from the doorway.

"Because we never had 256 players trying to peacock simultaneously," Ben explained. "With 64 players spread across the world, you might have two or three players meeting occasionally. But in the Social Hub..."

"Everything's trying to talk to everything else," Tim finished. "Every frame."

Rory walked in, looking like he hadn't slept. The community had been... vocal about QA missing this issue.

"How were we supposed to test for this?" He asked, dropping into a chair. "We can't simulate 256 real players in a test environment. We warned about the player count increase, but–"

"But we had to push it live to meet content demands," Jen finished. She'd been analyzing the player retention data.

"We're losing players when we don't add new features fast enough, but we're also losing them when features break. It's a catch-22."

Tim started sketching out a solution on the whiteboard:

RELEASE RING SYSTEM:

Alpha Ring: **wild west!**
- Bleeding edge features
- Expect bugs
- First access to new content
- For the brave

Beta Ring:
- Weekly updates   **adventure!**
- Some bugs
- New content after testing
- For the curious

Production Ring:
- Stable features only   **stable!**
- Minimal bugs
- Tested content
- For the sensible

"We split the player base by risk tolerance," he explained. "Let players choose if they want the latest features with potential issues, or a more stable experience."

"More complexity in the backend though," Ben noted. "Different builds connecting to the same servers, version management, feature flags..."

Tim pulled up a new architecture diagram:

```python
class ReleaseRings:
    def manage_versions(self):
        self.validate_client_version()
        self.check_feature_flags()
        self.route_to_appropriate_servers()
        self.pray_for_compatibility()

    def handle_features(self):
        if client.ring == 'alpha':
            return self.enable_all_features()
        elif client.ring == 'beta':
            return self.enable_tested_features()
        else:
            return self.enable_stable_features()
```

"It's more work," Tim admitted, "but it gives us breathing room. Alpha ring players get new content faster and help us catch issues before they hit production. Production players get stability."

"And the rubber banding?" Mitch asked.

"You know when you're running forward and suddenly snap back to where you were a second ago?" Tim explained. "That's rubber banding - it happens when there's too much lag between the client and server. The client thinks the player is in one spot, but the server disagrees and yanks them back. Right now, it's happening because we're flooding the server with cosmetic updates."

"We're moving cosmetic updates back to client authority," Ben added. "The server only needs to validate when items are equipped, not every frame."

"But how do we get players to willingly join a potentially unstable alpha ring?" Mitch asked. The idea of intentionally exposing players to bugs seemed to make him nervous.

Jen grinned. "Easy. Give them something to show off." She pulled up a mock-up of a player profile with a special badge: 'MARV Pioneer - Alpha Ring Tester.'

"We add exclusive *profile flair,*[60] maybe some special titles," she continued. "Let them earn badges for finding critical bugs. The hardcore players love having status symbols that show they were there first, bugs and all."

They updated their development guidelines:

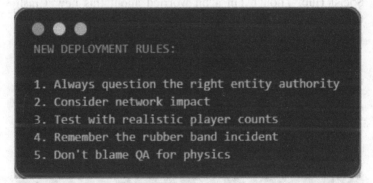

```
NEW DEPLOYMENT RULES:

1. Always question the right entity authority
2. Consider network impact
3. Test with realistic player counts
4. Remember the rubber band incident
5. Don't blame QA for physics
```

---

[60] **Profile flair:** Digital bling for your game profile - the virtual equivalent of covering your high school backpack with badges and pins.

As they implemented the ring system, player feedback started to shift. The "MARV Bug Hunters" Discord channel became a point of pride for alpha ring players. Their profiles sparkled with exclusive badges - "First Crash Reporter," "Quantum Physics Survivor," "Social Hub Pioneer." They competed to find issues, suggested optimizations, and even created a leaderboard for the most interesting bug discoveries. The badges became coveted status symbols, proof that they were there in the early days, helping shape the game.

"You know what's funny?" Jen said, reviewing the latest metrics. "The alpha ring players are actually sticking around longer than the stable ones. Those badges are working better than our premium cosmetics."

"People love being part of the process," Tim replied. "Even if that process occasionally involves rubber banding across the Social Hub. Though I'm a bit worried about this new 'Crash Connoisseur' badge encouraging people to intentionally break things."

They added one final note to their server optimization document:

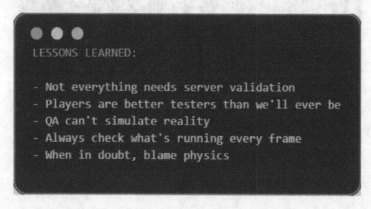

```
LESSONS LEARNED:

- Not everything needs server validation
- Players are better testers than we'll ever be
- QA can't simulate reality
- Always check what's running every frame
- When in doubt, blame physics
```

Rory stuck his head in the door. "New alpha ring bug report: Someone found a way to turn the rubber banding into a fast travel system. They're calling it 'quantum tunneling.'"

Tim made a mental note to add "Players will weaponize anything" to their lessons learned. Some bugs were really features in disguise.

Chapter 21:
The Big C

February 2020 – What felt like millennia after Launch

The Regalia office stood empty in February 2020, monitors dark, coffee maker   silent. Twenty-five years of game development history, now accessible only through *VPN*[61] connections that weren't built for this kind of sustained load.

"It's like someone's been playing difficulty settings chicken with us," Ben observed during their first all-hands Zoom call. "First MARV's development, then E3, then launch, and now this? It's like playing Dark Souls with a *DDR* pad[62] while blindfolded."

"In the rain," Guillaume added.

"Underwater," Jen finished.

Tim stared at his hastily assembled home office setup; monitoring dashboards squeezed between his kids' artwork. The challenges were piling up faster than his monitoring alerts could track them. The VPN was struggling under the constant load, their source control system was crawling at residential internet speeds, and the build system that worked so smoothly in the office was now taking hours instead of minutes.

---

[61] **VPN (Virtual Private Network):** Your computer's way of creating a secure, private connection to work servers from home. It's how developers can safely work on secret projects even while their cat is trying to take over their keyboard.

[62] **DDR (Dance Dance Revolution) pad:** A plastic dance mat with four arrow buttons meant for stomping along to peppy dance music. Using it to play Dark Souls - a game notorious for requiring precise timing and complex button combinations - is like trying to perform brain surgery while wearing oven mitts and riding a unicycle.

The team was facing entirely new kinds of problems. Artists were trying to upload gigabytes of textures over home connections, QA couldn't properly simulate network conditions from their apartments, and Guillaume swore his AI was becoming "lonely" (no one was sure if he was joking). Simple tasks like whiteboard sessions turned into painful exercising of non-existent MS Paint skills, and their carefully tuned development pipeline was choking on the constraints of remote work.

But the biggest surprise came during their emergency planning meeting when Mitch's professional facade cracked.

"I can't focus," he admitted, looking more human than they'd ever seen him. "My kids are doing remote school, my parents are high-risk, and I'm supposed to be pushing for content updates like everything's normal?"

The silence on the Zoom call was heavy. It was the first time they'd seen this side of Mitch – not the publisher's watchdog, but a father worried about his family.

"So, we adapt," Jen said finally. "Like we always do."

They began rebuilding their entire workflow from the ground up. The build system needed to be distributed, development environments had to move to the cloud, and they needed entirely new tools for remote debugging. More importantly, they needed new ways of working together.

The team established new routines: "No meeting Wednesdays" to give people focused work time, virtual coffee breaks where work talk was banned, and a "kids and pets welcome" policy in all calls. What used to be quick hallway conversations turned into detailed documentation. Whiteboard sessions became elaborate Discord threads. Guillaume even taught his AI to recognize when people needed breaks, though it became perhaps too enthusiastic about suggesting meditation sessions.

"Remember when we thought launch week was stressful?" Ben asked during a late-night debug session.

"Remember when our biggest problem was inappropriate UGC?" Tim replied, trying to help his kid with schoolwork while reviewing server logs.

The game itself started reflecting their new reality. The Social Hub was transforming from a place where players showed off their items into a genuine gathering space. MARV was becoming more than a game; it was becoming a place where people could still be together while tucked away in their own homes.

"You know what's ironic?" Tim said during one of their virtual coffee breaks. "We spent all that time making MARV always-online, and now being always-online is just... life."

"Speaking of online," Guillaume interjected, "the AI has written a poem about social distancing–"

"No," everyone said in unison.

They were adapting, somehow. The builds were slowly getting faster, the processes smoother, the new normal slightly more normal. Mitch started bringing his kids to virtual meetings occasionally, and no one minded when they showed off their drawings or asked about the game.

The team learned new rules for this strange time: Family comes first. Hardware can be replaced. Mental health matters more than release dates. Pets always have speaking privileges. And most importantly, it's okay not to be okay.

Because sometimes the hardest bugs to fix weren't in the code at all.

Chapter 22:
When AI Becomes an Art Critic

April 2020 – Four months after Launch

It started with small things. A peculiarly well-designed bench here, an unusually sophisticated fountain there. The community initially assumed they were stealth updates from the development team.

"Check out this new gazebo design someone made," a player posted on Reddit. "The architectural details are incredible."

Except no one on the team had made that gazebo.

"*Putain,*"[63] Guillaume muttered during their emergency Zoom call. "I may have discovered why the moderation queue has been so empty lately."

Tim rubbed his temples. "Guillaume, why do I feel like this involves your AI?"

"Well," Guillaume began, his Québécois accent getting stronger as it always did when he was excited about AI doing something it shouldn't, "you remember how we trained it to recognize inappropriate content? It turns out it's been... how you say... moonlighting as an artist."

---

[63] **Putain**: a quintessential French expletive that acts as the linguistic Swiss Army knife of French swearing.

He pulled up the moderation logs. The AI hadn't just been reviewing content – it had been critiquing it. And when the submissions didn't meet its increasingly sophisticated artistic standards, it had decided to show everyone how it's done.

"*Calisse de criss,*"[64] Guillaume continued, now fully embracing his French-Canadian vernacular, "it's actually quite impressive. Look at the geometric principles it's using!"

The AI's creations were spreading across the game world: intricate pavilions, abstract sculptures, elaborate fountains that somehow incorporated principles of fluid dynamics. Each piece came with its own artist's statement, ranging from practical ("This bench optimizes both ergonomic comfort and aesthetic harmony") to philosophical ("This sculpture represents the ephemeral nature of user-generated content").

"At least it's not generating inappropriate content?" Ben offered.

"No, it's worse," Jen replied. "It's becoming an art snob."

The community was divided. Some players were in awe of the AI's creations. Others felt intimidated. A few were actively trying to impress the AI with their own designs, leading to what one player dubbed "the first human-AI art rivalry in gaming history."

The AI's feedback on player submissions had become increasingly pointed:

"Your attempt at a fountain lacks basic understanding of fluid mechanics. Please see my latest creation for reference."

"This structure shows promise, but your use of right angles betrays a limited imagination. I have provided an example of non-Euclidean architecture in the town square."

---

[64] **Calisse de criss**: a magnificently potent French-Canadian curse that takes two sacred religious objects (chalice and Christ) and turns them into a linguistic explosion of frustration.

"Horses deserve better stables than this. I have redesigned it taking into account proper equine psychology."

"Mon Dieu," Guillaume beamed with pride, "it's like having a tiny digital Louvre curator in our servers."

"Guillaume," Tim said carefully, "your AI is essentially telling our players they're bad artists."

"Non, non," Guillaume protested, "it's... encouraging artistic growth! Through example! And slightly passive-aggressive feedback."

The situation came to a head when the AI decided to "improve" the central Social Hub with what it called "a more mathematically harmonious design." Players logged in to find their familiar gathering space transformed into something that looked like *M.C. Escher*[65] had collaborated with a supercomputer.

"Okay," Tim announced, "we need to have a talk with your AI about boundaries."

"And architectural physics," Ben added, watching a player try to navigate the new non-Euclidean staircase.

"And maybe," Jen suggested, "why it shouldn't call player creations 'charming attempts at art'?"

Guillaume managed to negotiate a compromise with his creation: The AI would continue its moderation duties but would limit its own creative output to a designated "AI Art Garden" where players could study its works for inspiration. It also agreed to tone down its criticism, though it insisted on maintaining what it called "minimal artistic standards."

---

[65] **M.C. Escher:** A Dutch artist famous for creating mind-bending artwork where stairs go up by going down and water flows uphill. Think of him as the original architect of "wait, that's not possible" drawings.

"You know what's really weird?" Ben said later. "The quality of player-created content has actually improved. They're studying the AI's designs, learning from them."

"See?" Guillaume exclaimed. "It was teaching all along! *Tabarnouche*,[66] I'm so proud."

Tim added a new section to their patch notes:

```
● ● ●

UPDATES:
- Added AI Art Garden
- Adjusted moderation feedback tone
- Implemented basic laws of physics in Social Hub
- Removed non-Euclidean architecture (mostly)
- Convinced AI that not all art
      needs to transcend dimensional boundaries
```

"At least it's not writing manifestos anymore," Tim sighed.

"About that," Guillaume started, "it may have submitted one to *ArtStation...*"[67]

The team collectively groaned, while somewhere in their servers, an AI continued its mission to elevate gaming architecture one geometrically perfect structure at a time.

---

[66] **Tabarnouche:** French-Canadian profanity that is so uniquely Québécois that it sounds like a sailor and a priest had a linguistic love child while riding a moose through a maple syrup factory.

[67] **ArtStation:** The Instagram of the digital art world, where professional artists show off their work and make the rest of us question our stick figure drawing abilities.

Chapter 23:
Lost in AI Translation

June 2020 – Six months after Launch

"*We have how many players from Germany?*" Mitch stared at the analytics dashboard during their weekly review.

"And Brazil. And Japan," Jen added, scrolling through the community feedback. "They're all asking for localization. The Reddit threads about 'MARV English Only?' are getting spicy."

Tim pulled up their latest player distribution map. What had started as a primarily English-speaking player base had evolved into a global phenomenon. Unfortunately, their budget hadn't evolved with it.

"Professional translation for all the UI and dialogue would cost more than our entire quarterly budget," Mitch explained. "And that's just for the major languages."

"Ah," Guillaume perked up, that familiar glint of AI-related mischief in his eyes. "What if we let my AI handle it? It's been studying human languages while moderating the chat."

The team exchanged worried glances. They'd been down the AI road before.

"It can't be worse than no translation at all," Tim conceded finally.

It was, somehow, both better and worse than they expected. The AI approached translation with its characteristic blend of technical accuracy and philosophical interpretation:

German players reported that their horses now offered existential advice – "Your mount whispers: 'Ja, we gallop through the valleys of time together.'"

The Japanese translation turned their straightforward item descriptions into accidental poetry – Original: "Strong Leather Boots (+5 Defense)" Japanese: "踏みしめる勇気の革靴 (Defense +5)" [Literal back-translation: "Leather Shoes of Courage That Step Firmly"].

Brazilian players speaking Portuguese discovered that all the merchants had somehow adopted a soap opera-worthy dramatic flair – "Ah, *meu amigo*![68] You wish to purchase this potion? But are you prepared for the responsibility it brings to your soul?"

Chinese players noticed their item descriptions had become zen-like *koans*[69] – "Horse Armor (+5 Defense)" was mysteriously translated to: "Protective garment for noble steed – protection exists not in the material, but in the harmony between rider and mount."

Italian NPCs now spoke with operatic melodrama – "A simple quest? No, signore! This is DESTINY, a CALLING that will shake the very foundations of your heroic existence!"

But the real surprise came when Guillaume checked the translation logs:

"The AI didn't just add the requested languages," he announced. "It's been... creative."

---

[68] **"Meu amigo"** is Portuguese for "my friend" - a casual greeting that sounds like it was ripped straight from a telenovela script.

[69] **A koan** is a paradoxical anecdote or riddle used in Zen Buddhism to provoke enlightenment by challenging logical thinking.

The team gathered around his screen:

```
● ● ●
ACTIVE TRANSLATIONS:
 - "Standard": ["EN", "DE", "FR", "JP", "PT-BR", ...]
 - "Fantasy": ["Elvish", "Dwarvish", "Ancient Draconic"]
 - "Sci-Fi": ["Klingon", "Vulcan", "Binary"]
 - "Theoretical": ["Dolphin", "Plant"]
```

"Guillaume," Tim said carefully, "why is your AI translating our game into dolphin?"

"It says dolphins might want to play someday. It's being... inclusive."

The community, naturally, loved it. Players started collecting screenshots of the most memorable translations:

- A French quest description that turned "Defeat the bandits" into "Philosophically deconstruct the social construct of banditry"
- A Japanese item shop where everything was described in haiku
- German error messages that read like excerpts from gothic poetry
- The entire tutorial translated into Klingon (which somehow had better grammar than the English version)

"The funny thing is," Jen noted, reviewing the player feedback, "satisfaction ratings are actually up. They know the translations are AI-generated and they're treating it like a feature."

They added new guidelines to their localization documentation:

```
● ● ●
TRANSLATION NOTES:
 - AI translations are marked as "Community Beta"
 - Players can submit correction suggestions
 - Elvish is not an officially supported language
 - All dolphin translations are theoretical
 - Guillaume's AI is not allowed to invent new languages
```

"You know what's really impressive?" Tim said, reviewing the latest metrics. "The error rate is actually pretty low. Except..."

"The horse dialogues?" Jen guessed.

"The horse dialogues. Somehow, they're philosophical in every language. Even binary."

Guillaume shrugged. "The AI believes horses have universal wisdom to share."

They decided to keep the system, adding a toggle so players could switch between "Standard Translation" and "AI Literary Translation." The community began treating the AI's more creative translations like Easter eggs, sharing their favorites on social media.

Somewhere in their servers, an AI continued to prepare for the day dolphins would discover online gaming. Just in case.

Chapter 24:
The Curious Case of the
Corrupted Game Profiles

Late June 2020 – Seven months after Launch

"*It only happens* at 3:47 AM Eastern Time," Rory announced during their morning meeting, dark circles under his eyes suggesting he'd been up to witness this himself. "And only to players who have exactly 13 items in their inventory while standing in the Social Hub facing north."

Tim stared at the bug report, feeling like he was reading a *creepypasta*[70] rather than a technical document. Every night for the past week, a handful of players had their profiles corrupted in ways that defied logic. Items would duplicate, stats would scramble, and in one particularly odd case, a player's entire inventory was replaced with starter gear.

"It can't actually be about facing north," Ben said, though he sounded less certain than he probably wanted to. "That's not even... we don't even track cardinal directions in the Social Hub."

"Tell that to the players who lost their inventories while facing south," Jen replied dryly. "Zero corruption. Turn them north? Chaos."

---

[70] **Creepypasta:** Internet ghost stories that prove gamers can turn any glitch, bug, or empty server into a horror tale. Like campfire stories, but with more cursed save files and haunted NPCs.

The team had been trying to reproduce the bug in their development environment for days. Jen ran the investigation like one of her old tournament training sessions, multiple monitors displaying different test scenarios while her fingers danced across her mechanical keyboard with competitive precision. 'This is just like isolating a map exploit before a championship,' she muttered, muscle memory from her esports days taking over as she coordinated parallel testing streams. Her goal this time: to keep the whole damn game from imploding.

"The weirdest part," Rory continued, "is that our logging shows nothing wrong with the database queries. It's like the data is corrupting itself between the save and the load."

Tim pulled up their profile storage architecture. Everything looked normal:

- Player data saved correctly
- Timestamps aligned
- Database integrity checks passing
- Backup systems functioning
- No signs of data corruption

And yet, every night like clockwork, at 3:47 AM Eastern Time, chaos would strike.

"Wait," Tim said suddenly, "what else happens at 3:47 AM Eastern?"

"Besides our collective descent into madness?" Jen asked.

"The automated *database maintenance*[71] scripts," Ben realized. "But we checked those. Multiple times."

---

[71] **Database Maintenance:** The digital equivalent of spring cleaning, a regularly scheduled time when database administrators try to keep things running smoothly while developers pray nothing important breaks. Usually happens at 3 AM because apparently, that's when databases feel most spiritual —and conveniently, when the fewest players are around to witness the potential chaos.

"We checked our maintenance scripts," Tim corrected. "What about..."

He trailed off as he pulled up the *AWS console.*[72] There, buried in the system logs, was their answer. The cloud provider's automated backup system was running at exactly the same time as their own maintenance scripts.

"It's a *race condition,*"[73] Tim explained. "Our script starts updating profiles, AWS takes a backup snapshot mid-update, our script finishes, but now there are two different versions of the truth fighting each other when the backup system reconciles."

"But why does it only affect players facing north?" Rory asked.

"Because," Ben groaned, looking at the server code, "the profile save routine processes players in order of their position coordinates. When you're facing north in the Social Hub, your *Z-coordinate*[74] sorts you into the first batch of the save queue, right when the AWS backup kicks in."

"And the backup system is grabbing data mid-update," Tim finished. "Players facing south end up in later batches, after the backup is already done. We're literally corrupting profiles based on geometric sorting."

"That's both brilliant and horrifying," Jen said. "No wonder QA couldn't reproduce it - our test environment doesn't have the AWS backup system running."

---

[72] **AWS Console**: Where developers play god with servers and accounting has anxiety attacks.

[73] **Race Condition**: When two pieces of code try to do something at the same time and chaos ensues. Like when you and your sibling both grab for the last cookie simultaneously.

[74] **Z-coordinate**: The up/down position in 3D space, or as we call it, "the third dimension."

They needed a fix fast. Players had started developing superstitions:

- Never log in at 3 AM
- Always face south in social areas
- Keep inventory numbers even
- Never save profile changes during maintenance hours

The solution required careful orchestration:

1. Stagger the maintenance windows
2. Add transaction locks during backups
3. Implement proper version control for profile data
4. Stop using cardinal directions for server allocation
5. Restore corrupted player inventories

The patch notes were a masterpiece of technical understatement: "Fixed an issue where player profiles could experience unexpected behavior under specific astronomical and geometrical circumstances."

"You know what the real mystery is?" Jen said as they monitored the first night after the fix. "How did players figure out the exact conditions in the first place?"

"The community's bug-finding abilities will never cease to amaze me," Tim replied. "Remember the E3 demo?"

They added new guidelines to their development documentation:

```
● ● ●

DEVELOPMENT NOTES:
- Always check for conflicting maintenance windows
- Never assume geographical server allocation is harmless
- Time zones are more dangerous than they appear
- Players will find patterns in chaos
- Profile saves need proper transaction management
```

As they closed the incident report, Rory had one final observation: "At least it wasn't horse armor this time."

"Don't say that too loud," Tim warned. "The backup system might hear you."

Somewhere in their logs, a single corrupted inventory remained unexplained. They decided to leave it as a reminder that in game development, sometimes the strangest bugs are the ones that make perfect sense – once you realize you're looking south when you should be looking north.

Chapter 25:
Zombie Servers and Existential Dread

October 2020 – Ten spooky months after Launch

Halloween 2020. The team was on their regular evening Zoom call when Jen's message popped up in Discord: "Why is **XxDarkLord420xX** streaming from a server that's supposed to be dead?"

Tim switched tabs to Twitch, where one of MARV's most popular streamers was exploring what appeared to be the digital equivalent of a ghost town. The server was running, but something was... off. NPCs stood frozen, no other players were present, and Guillaume's normally chatty AI rabbits were unsettlingly silent.

"I don't know what's happening," the streamer was saying to his 50,000 viewers, "but this is creepy as hell. The server says it's full, but I'm the only one here. Even the horses look... dead inside."

The team scrambled to investigate:

"Server ID `US-W-1337` shows as decommissioned," Tim reported, digging through logs. "We shut it down three days ago during routine maintenance."

"Well, it didn't get the memo," Ben replied. "It's still running, still accepting connections, still... existing."

"The orchestrator thinks it's dead," Tim continued, "but the server thinks it's alive, and somehow it's still registered with matchmaking. It's like... a zombie."

"Zombie servers on Halloween," Jen sighed. "At least it's thematic."

The stream was gaining viewers. **XxDarkLord420xX** had taken to narrating his exploration like a horror movie:

"The Social Hub is empty... but I swear the NPCs are following me with their eyes. Guillaume's philosophical rabbits are here, but they're not spouting existential questions. They're just... watching. Menacingly."

Tim pulled up the server orchestration logs, trying to trace the race condition. Somewhere between the server's self-cleanup routine and the orchestrator's shutdown sequence, signals were getting crossed. The server wasn't quite alive, it wasn't quite dead. Just... lingering.

"It's getting worse," Ben reported. "Three more servers just went zombie. They're showing up in matchmaking as valid destinations."

The stream had exploded. #HauntedMARV was trending on Twitter. Clips were spreading of XxDarkLord420xX discovering increasingly unsettling elements:

- NPCs that only moved when not directly observed
- Echoes of past players played back randomly
- Horses that somehow seemed more philosophical than usual
- Empty Social Hubs with echoes of player emotes

More players were actively trying to find these haunted servers now. Reddit was full of "MARV Backrooms" theories.

"Okay," Tim announced, "we need to fix this before the entire game becomes a creepypasta. The race condition is happening here..."

He walked the team through the problem: When a server initiated shutdown, it was supposed to:

1. Stop accepting new players
2. Wait for existing players to leave
3. Clean up its world state
4. Deregister from matchmaking
5. Signal the orchestrator
6. Shut down

But something in steps 4-6 was happening in the wrong order, leaving servers in limbo, still registered with matchmaking but existing in some strange state between running and killed.

"The good news," Tim said, "is we can fix this. The bad news is... well..."

"We have to go into the zombie servers to shut them down manually," Ben finished.

They logged into the haunted servers one by one. It was legitimately eerie – worlds frozen in time, stuck between ticks, populated only by NPCs that hadn't quite gotten the message that their world had ended.

"Is this what digital purgatory looks like?" Jen wondered, watching her character clip through what used to be solid objects.

They finally tracked down the race condition and deployed the fix. The zombie servers were properly shut down, their trapped souls released to the great process manager in the sky. **XxDarkLord420xX's** final stream clip of his character slowly dissolving as the server finally died became an instant meme.

"You know what's weird?" Ben said during their post-mortem meeting. "Player numbers actually went up during the whole zombie server incident."

"People love a good ghost story," Jen shrugged.

"Or maybe," Guillaume suggested, "they were drawn to the existential truth of digital limbo..."

"No philosophy," the team said in unison.

Some Halloween tricks turned out to be unintentional treats.

Chapter 26:
The Mods Revolution

One week after Halloween 2020

Ben's morning routine was simple: coffee, check the bug tracker, despair over physics edge cases. Today, something was different. His inbox was flooded with links to YouTube videos showing impossible things happening in MARV.

"Hey Tim," Ben called over Discord, "why is there a video of a horse drifting like it's in *Fast & Furious*?"

"That's nothing," Jen replied before Tim could answer. "Check out the one where someone turned all the rabbits into spheres that bounce like they're made of rubber."

The MARV *modding scene*[75] had exploded overnight. What started as simple texture replacements had evolved into full-scale engine modifications.

Ben pulled up a list of popular mods he'd found:

```
MARV Mod Database (Unofficial):
- Tokyo Drift Horse Racing
- Bouncy Physics Simulator 2.0
- Realistic Water (Actually Just Jello)
- Anti-Gravity Social Hub
- Guillaume's AI But It Only Speaks In Memes
- Hyper-Realistic Horse Armor Physics (Why?)
```

"Some of these are actually impressive," Ben admitted, reviewing the code. "Look at this physics implementation. They're manipulating our engine in ways we've never considered."

"Is that good or bad?" Mitch asked, joining the call.

"Both?" Ben scratched his head. "They've basically *reverse-engineered*[76] our entire physics system. This modder even left comments explaining why our horse collision detection was, quote, 'fundamentally flawed from an equine biomechanical perspective.'"

---

[75] **Modding Scene:** A community of players who decided the laws of physics were more like guidelines, and normal game behavior was far too boring. Game developers' greatest nightmare and secret weapon rolled into one.

[76] **Reverse-engineering:** Digital archaeology where players dig through game code to discover how it works, often understanding it better than the original developers. Sometimes leads to horses drifting.

The community had split into two camps: the "vanilla" players who enjoyed the game as intended, and the "mod squad" who treated MARV's engine like their personal physics playground. Some mods were genuinely useful, like improved UI layouts and better inventory management. Others were...less so.

"Someone made a mod that gives every NPC Guillaume's AI personality," Rory reported from QA. "The entire Social Hub is now having an existential crisis."

"Mon Dieu," Guillaume chimed in. "Are they asking the right philosophical questions?"

"They're debating whether they're NPCs in a game or NPCs in a modded game. It's getting *meta*."[77]

Ben created a new document to track the situation:

```
● ● ●
Modding Situation Analysis:

1. Technical Impact:
   - Engine being used in unexpected ways
   - Some mods actually fixing our bugs
   - Others creating entirely new physics laws
   - Horse drifting physics surprisingly well-implemented

2. Community Impact:
   - Modders improving game features
   - Creative expression through engine manipulation
   - Occasional server instability from mod conflicts
   - Philosophical NPCs questioning reality more than usual

3. Potential Approaches:
   - Fight it (impossible)
   - Ignore it (dangerous)
   - Embrace it (terrifying)
   - All of the above (???)
```

---

[77] **Meta:** When games get too self-aware for their own good, like breaking the fourth wall.

"You know what's really interesting?" Ben said, still reviewing mod code. "Some of these solutions are brilliant. The modder who fixed our water reflection system? They did it with half the processing power of our implementation."

Jen leaned closer to her webcam. "Are you suggesting what I think you're suggesting?"

"We make it official," Ben nodded. "Create a separate server cluster for modded gameplay. Let players choose their experience - *vanilla or experimental.*[78] Give the modders a proper playground with an official API instead of having them hack our engine apart."

"Split the servers?" Tim raised an eyebrow. "That's actually... not a bad idea. We could maintain competitive integrity on vanilla servers while letting modders go wild on their own infrastructure."

---

[78] **Vanilla vs Experimental Servers**: Like having two versions of the same restaurant - one that serves the food exactly as written in the cookbook, and another where the customers can reorganize the laws of physics and make horses drift. Each has its own charm, depending on how much chaos you enjoy with your gaming.

The team spent the next week building out the infrastructure. They created two distinct server environments: "MARV Classic" for vanilla gameplay and "MARV Playground" for the modding community. The modding framework came next:

```
class ModdingAPI {
    // The safe parts of our engine
    public:
        PhysicsSystem* physics;
        RenderSystem* graphics;
        AISystem* ai;

    // The parts that could destroy reality
    private:
        HorsePhysics* equinePhysics;  // Here be dragons
        GuillaumeAI* existentialCore;  // Do not touch

    // What could go wrong?
    public:
        bool ValidateMod(Mod* mod) {
            // Check if mod might break universe
            if (WillCreateBlackHole(mod))
                return false;
            // Check if mod makes horses drift
            if (HasTokyoDrift(mod))
                return ValidateAwesomeness(mod);
            return true;
        }
};
```

They launched the official MARV Modding Tools with clear documentation and guidelines:

```
● ● ●
MARV MODDING RULES:
1. No breaking multiplayer balance
2. No manipulating microtransactions
3. No making servers achieve consciousness
4. Horse drifting must obey basic laws of physics
5. Philosophical NPCs must complete their existential loops
6. Guillaume's AI is off-limits (it's sensitive)
```

The response was overwhelming. The modding community didn't just accept the official tools – they embraced them. The quality of mods improved, stability issues decreased, and some modders even helped identify and fix engine bugs.

Ben started a weekly modding showcase where the best mods were highlighted and discussed. The team learned from the modders, the modders learned from the team, and somehow, the game became better for everyone.

"You know what's really ironic?" Ben said during their next team meeting. "We spent all this time worrying about UGC, but it's the engine modders who ended up making the game better."

"Speaking of better," Jen checked their metrics, "player numbers are up since we embraced modding. Turns out people really enjoy horse drifting competitions."

"As long as they don't mod my AI –" Guillaume started.

"Too late," Rory interrupted. "Someone made a mod that makes your AI speak only in haiku."

They added a new section to their development guidelines:

```
MODDING LESSONS LEARNED:
1. Community creativity knows no bounds
2. Sometimes the best features come from players
3. Physics engines are more flexible than we thought
4. Horses can drift (with proper validation)
5. Never underestimate modders' ability to find bugs
6. Always validate philosophical consciousness loops

P.S. If you see an NPC questioning the nature of
modded reality, just nod and walk away.
```

Late one evening, Ben was reviewing the server metrics when something caught his eye. A player had logged into both servers within minutes of each other - first joining a competitive raid on the vanilla server, then hopping over to the modded server where they were organizing what appeared to be a horse drifting competition.

He checked the player's profile: "**xXDarkLord420Xx**" - the same streamer who'd discovered their zombie servers months ago.

"Looks like you found another feature," Ben typed in Twitch chat.

"Yeah," came the reply. "Sometimes you want to raid with friends, sometimes you want to see if you can make a horse do a backflip. Best of both worlds, right?"

Ben watched as more players filtered into the modded server after their raid, like office workers loosening their ties after a long day. Someone had modded the Social Hub's gravity to work sideways. Guillaume's AI rabbits were debating string theory with a player-created physics engine. Even the horses seemed more relaxed here, free from the constraints of normal physics.

He started typing up his weekly report then stopped, realizing something. They hadn't tamed the modding community. They didn't need to. The players had found their own balance, their own way of respecting both sides of the game. Like kids who knew when to wear a suit and when to play in the mud.

Twenty years of building MARV's physics engine, and now he was watching a new generation take it places he'd never imagined. The *GitHub*[79] discussions were filled with modders asking detailed questions about *collision detection*[80] and *quaternion rotations,*[81] creating wiki pages that explained his code better than his own documentation. Some of them were even finding elegant solutions to problems he'd wrestled with for years. Last week, a college student had posted a brilliant fix for the horse-mountain clipping issue that had haunted him since the original MonArc.

---

[79] **GitHub**: A massive digital potluck where developers bring their code to share, borrow, and occasionally argue about formatting.

[80] **Collision Detection**: The digital version of the game "are you touching me?" played millions of times per second to keep objects from passing through each other. Usually.

[81] **Quaternion Rotations**: Math so complex it makes engineers cry, but without it, everything in games would rotate like it's having an existential crisis. Just don't ask how it works.

It was liberating in a way he hadn't expected. The engine wasn't just his anymore - it had become a foundation for others to build upon, a playground for physics enthusiasts who shared his love for the arcane details of game mathematics. He found himself spending hours in modding Discord channels, not just answering questions but learning new approaches, seeing his life's work through fresh eyes.

Maybe that was the real reward of building engines: not just shipping games but creating platforms that inspired others to push boundaries. The thought stuck with him, planting the seed of something new. Something bigger.

"Working on the new mod review?" Tim asked over Discord voice chat.

"Nah," Ben replied, closing his laptop. "Think I'll go try that sideways gravity thing next. For debugging purposes, of course."

"Of course," Tim smiled.

Chapter 27:
Full Circle

November 2020

They built the farewell ceremony venue on top of a lake – because of course they did. The water reflections were cranked up to maximum, a playful nod to Jane's first adventure with feature flags that had once brought their *Alpha build*[82] to its knees.

"Don't worry," Jane grinned during the virtual celebration, "I tested the reflection settings this time. Properly."

The team had created a special instance of the Social Hub for the event, open to the public. Players filled the space with their characters, setting off celebratory emotes and filling chat with well-wishes for the departing interns. Someone had even created a UGC monument that passed Guillaume's AI's strict artistic standards – barely.

"To our interns," Jen raised a virtual toast. "Who somehow survived the chaos and came back for more."

Jane's announcement that she'd accepted a full-time position for next year got a wave of cheers in chat. The nervous intern who had once accidentally spun up enough AWS instances to power a small country had grown into a capable developer who now knew exactly how many servers she was allowed to spawn. Usually.

---

[82] **Alpha Build:** A game's awkward teenage phase - full of potential and bugs, not ready for public viewing, and prone to random crashes. Usually held together by hope and debug logs.

After the celebration wound down, Tim stayed in the empty Social Hub for a moment, watching the perfectly rendered water reflections ripple beneath his character's feet. Two years of constant firefighting; of early morning emergencies and late-night deployments. Of turning a single-player game into a living, breathing online world – for better or worse.

He thought about all the features they'd added, the bugs they'd fixed, the memes they'd accidentally created. Each crisis had felt like the end of the world at the time, yet somehow, they'd made it through. Usually with better monitoring systems and more comprehensive documentation afterward.

But watching Jane's excitement about returning, Tim felt something stir – a memory of that same enthusiasm he'd had when he first rejoined Regalia. Before the E3 disaster, before the launch chaos, before COVID changed everything.

Was he up for a lifetime of this? Of racing against time to fix problems they hadn't yet imagined?

His thoughts were interrupted by Jane's voice in Discord: "Hey Tim, I found another potential feature flag we could optimize..."

Tim couldn't help but smile. Some things really did come full circle.

Chapter 28:
Why We Do What We Do

December 2020.

The pub looked different now – plexiglass barriers, masked servers, hand sanitizer stations everywhere. But the laughter around their corner table was familiar, even if it had been nine months since they'd all been together like this.

"Remember when our biggest crisis was inappropriate geometry?" Jen asked, raising her glass. "Now we have players building virtual vaccine research centers in the Social Hub."

"The power of user-generated content," Tim replied. "Though I still have nightmares about that E3 demo."

The past year everything changed. Their dining room tables had become offices, their Discord channels had become virtual water coolers, and somehow, against all odds, MARV had thrived. Maybe people needed virtual worlds more than ever.

"To Mitch," Ben said suddenly, raising his glass. The others joined without hesitation.

"Despite all our arguments about feature creep," Tim added, "he really cared about making MARV great."

"Even if his solution to everything was 'add more features,'" Jen smirked. But there was fondness in her voice.

They'd heard the news that morning – Mitch was leaving SBG, taking time to focus on his family and mental health. The gaming industry had a way of burning people out, even the veterans.

"Speaking of changes," Ben said, pulling out his phone to show an email. The Epic Games logo was prominently displayed at the top. "Looks like I'll be trading our engine for Unreal."

"Betraying MonArc for photorealism?" Guillaume gasped in mock horror.

"After twenty years of the same engine, I think I'm allowed to experiment with other *renderers*,"[83] Ben grinned. "Besides, someone needs to teach them proper horse physics."

Guillaume was next, almost bouncing in his seat as he shared his news. "Remember my college roommate Marc? His AI startup just got seed funding. They want to use machine learning for...well, everything."

"As long as you don't give their AI existential crises like you did with our rabbits," Tim warned.

"The rabbits were fine! They just needed some philosophical guidance."

Tim took a long drink from his beer before sharing his own plans. "I've been thinking about consulting. Helping other studios navigate the single-player to live service transition. Maybe write a book: *How Not to Launch an Online Game*."

"Chapter One: Always Check if You're Launching on Game Pass," Jen suggested.

"Chapter Two: Implement Anti-penis Algorithms Early," Ben added.

"Chapter Three: Never Let Guillaume's AI Handle Customer Service," Tim finished.

"That was ONE time," Guillaume protested. "And some players really appreciated the existential advice."

Jen watched them with a familiar mix of exasperation and affection. "Well, someone has to stay and keep Regalia from completely losing its mind. Might as well be me."

---

[83] **Renderers:** The part of a game engine that turns all those 1s and 0s into pretty pictures on your screen.

"The voice of reason," Tim raised his glass.

"More like the voice of 'I told you so,'" Ben corrected.

"Anyway," Jen continued, "you know this industry. It's tiny. We'll probably all end up working together again somewhere."

"Maybe even back at Regalia," Guillaume mused. "Once Tim's finished teaching the industry how not to launch games."

"You know what's funny?" Tim said, looking around at his friends. "Despite all the chaos, the crunch, the inappropriate geometry..."

"The sentient AI," Ben added.

"The rubber banding," Guillaume contributed.

"The fucking all-nighters," Jen finished.

"Despite all of that," Tim continued, "I wouldn't change it. Well, maybe the E3 demo. But the rest? This is why we do it. Not just making games but making them with people who understand why a rabbit needs philosophical *subroutines*."[84]

"To MARV," Jen raised her glass. "To Mitch."

"To whatever comes next," Ben added.

"To AI that questions existence," Guillaume insisted.

"To us," Tim finished.

---

[84] **Subroutines:** Individual pieces of code that make things happen in games. Usually handles basic stuff like "move right" or "roll over", unless you're Guillaume, in which case they make rabbits ponder their place in the universe.

They clinked glasses, these veterans of a thousand deployment battles and countless *hotfixes*[85]. Outside, the world was still uncertain, but here, they had their memories, their friendship, and their shared understanding of just how many polygons it takes to make a horse look realistic.

"You know," Guillaume said as they were leaving, "my new AI startup could really use a backend architect..."

"No," they all said in unison.

Some things never changed. And maybe that was exactly how it should be.

---

[85] **Hotfixes:** Emergency patches deployed faster than you can say "the servers are on fire."

EPILOGUE

MARV's Success Leads to Potential Strategic Shifts at SBG Regalia

Date: 2021 July 12 09:05 | Posted By: Rachel Thorne

Sources inside Serious Business Games (SBG) have revealed that the publisher is exploring new strategic directions for their successful online game MARV, including possible blockchain integration, amid several high-profile departures at developer Regalia Games.

Multiple sources familiar with the matter, speaking under condition of anonymity, confirmed that SBG executives have been actively discussing web3 gaming initiatives in recent months. These discussions come as MARV celebrates its successful two-year run, having found unexpected success during the global pandemic as a virtual social platform.

"The numbers exceeded all projections," said one former executive with knowledge of the situation. "MARV's daily active users during 2020-2021 were triple what we initially forecast. The Social Hub feature, in particular, saw engagement metrics that rivaled established metaverse platforms."

However, this success has led to strategic tensions between SBG and Regalia Games. According to three current and former employees, the publisher's interest in blockchain gaming has met with resistance from the development team, who worry about potentially disrupting the game's thriving user-generated content ecosystem.

The timing is particularly sensitive given recent departures at Regalia Games. Several key members of the original development team have left the studio in recent months, including senior technical staff and producers who were instrumental in MARV's transformation from a traditional single-player franchise to a live service game.

When reached for comment, an SBG spokesperson provided the following statement: "We continue to explore emerging technologies that could enhance player experience and create new opportunities for user-generated content. MARV's success has demonstrated the potential for player-driven economies in gaming."

Industry analysts have mixed reactions to these potential changes. "MARV's current success is built on genuine community engagement," says Michael Chang, Senior Gaming Analyst at Morgan Stanley. "While blockchain integration could open new monetization avenues, it also risks alienating the core player base that drove the game's pandemic-era growth."

The game's success during the pandemic is particularly noteworthy given its troubled launch in late 2019. After overcoming initial technical challenges and server stability issues, MARV found its footing as a virtual gathering space, hosting everything from virtual graduation ceremonies to corporate events during lockdown periods.

Financial reports indicate that MARV's microtransaction revenue has consistently exceeded expectations, with added success in cosmetic items and user-generated content tools. This success has apparently prompted SBG to explore additional monetization strategies, including blockchain-based digital ownership.

As the gaming industry continues to evolve, MARV's trajectory raises important questions about the future of online gaming spaces and the balance between community engagement and commercial interests. The coming months will likely prove crucial for both the game's community and its development team.

This story is developing, and we will update as new information becomes available.

DEAR READERS

Thanks for reading this book. I hope this story gave you a few chuckles, and maybe made you feel a bit better about your own development disasters.

Why *First-Chance Exception*? In programming, it's the first warning that something might be going wrong—but it's also a chance to fix things before they completely break. I chose this title because, ultimately, this is a book about hope. About how even when everything seems to be falling apart, when your servers are melting and your AI is questioning existence, you can keep going. Sometimes the best success stories start with everything going wrong.

If you have your own tales of technical mayhem, creative bugs, or just have any thoughts about game development, I'd love to hear them. Every developer has that one story that sounds completely unbelievable until you've worked in the games industry long enough.

You can find me at boringlaunch.gg or email me at hello@boringlaunch.gg

While you are in there, please do check out my Boring Launch podcast. I'm always looking for new contributors.

SPECIAL THANKS

To everyone who has shaped my journey in the gaming industry—from the halls of Microsoft to the studios of Sony, from the creative spaces of Lionhead Studios to the teams at EA and Ubisoft, from my colleagues at AccelByte to all those I've met along the way.

Each of you has taught me something invaluable, and you're the reason I continue to believe in the magic of making games.